This coloring book belongs to

AF231193

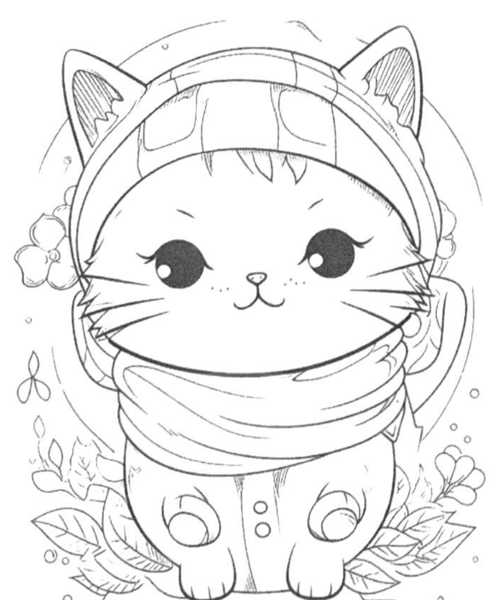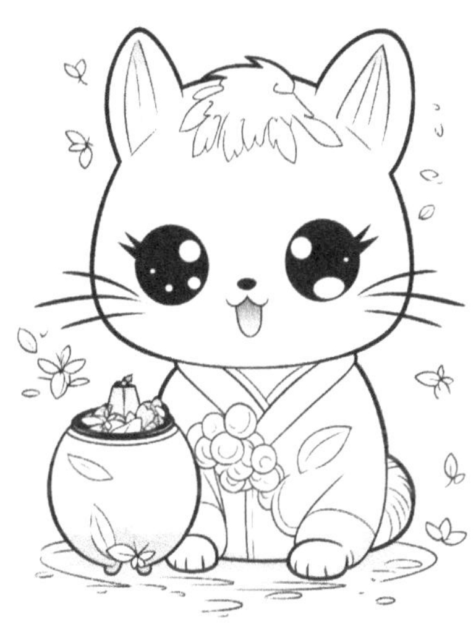

Love this Coloring book?
Want to show off your masterpiece?
Do you want your art displayed on our website?

1. Take a picture of a finished coloring page
2. Scan the QR Code to go to our website
3. Upload the photo of your finished coloring page

OR

Use #happytimesbooks or mention us @happytimesbooks on Instragram to have it displayed on our front page

No registration required

If you are under 18 please get a parents permission

https://happytimesbooks.com/pages/customer-art

Color Test Page

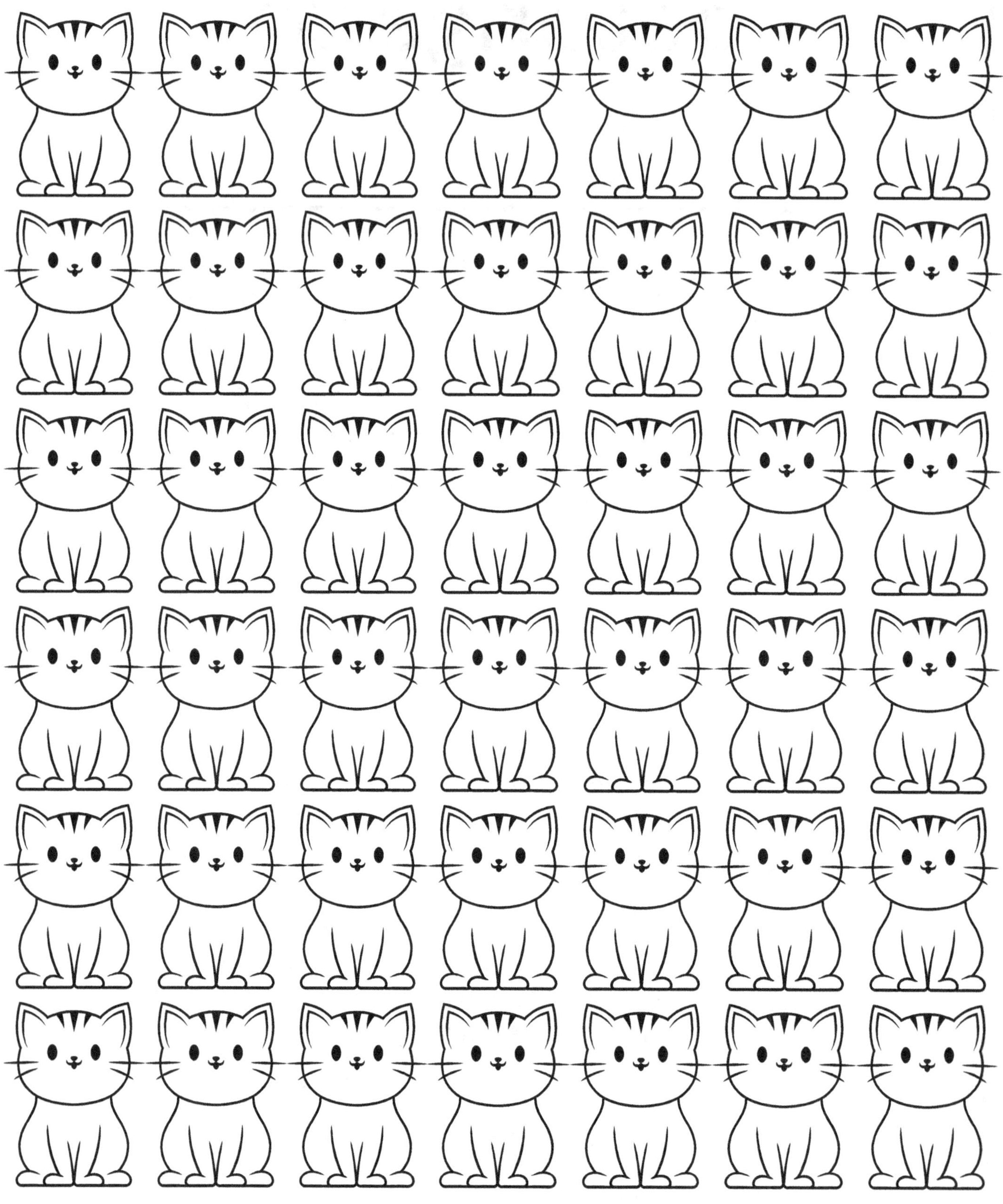

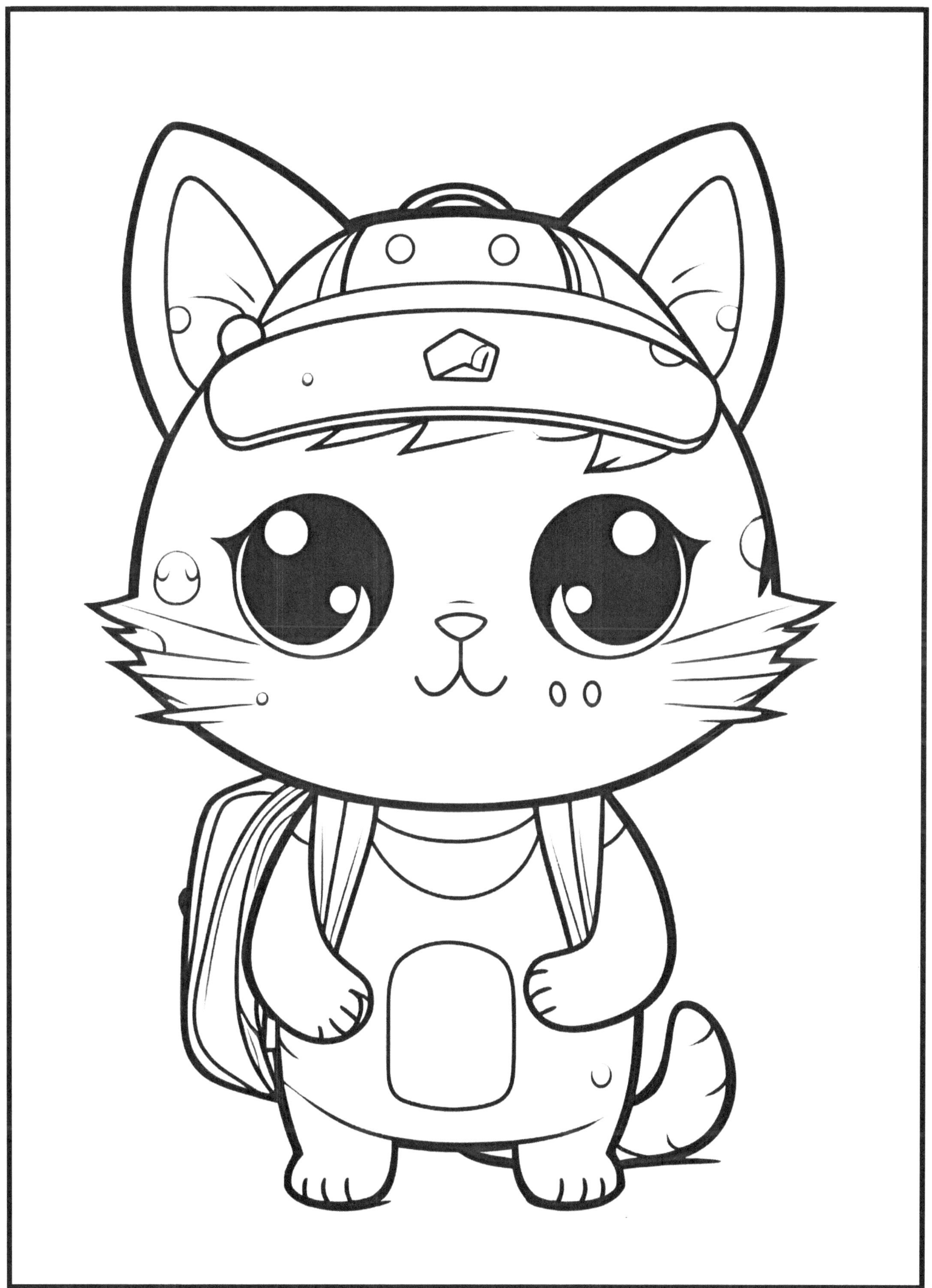

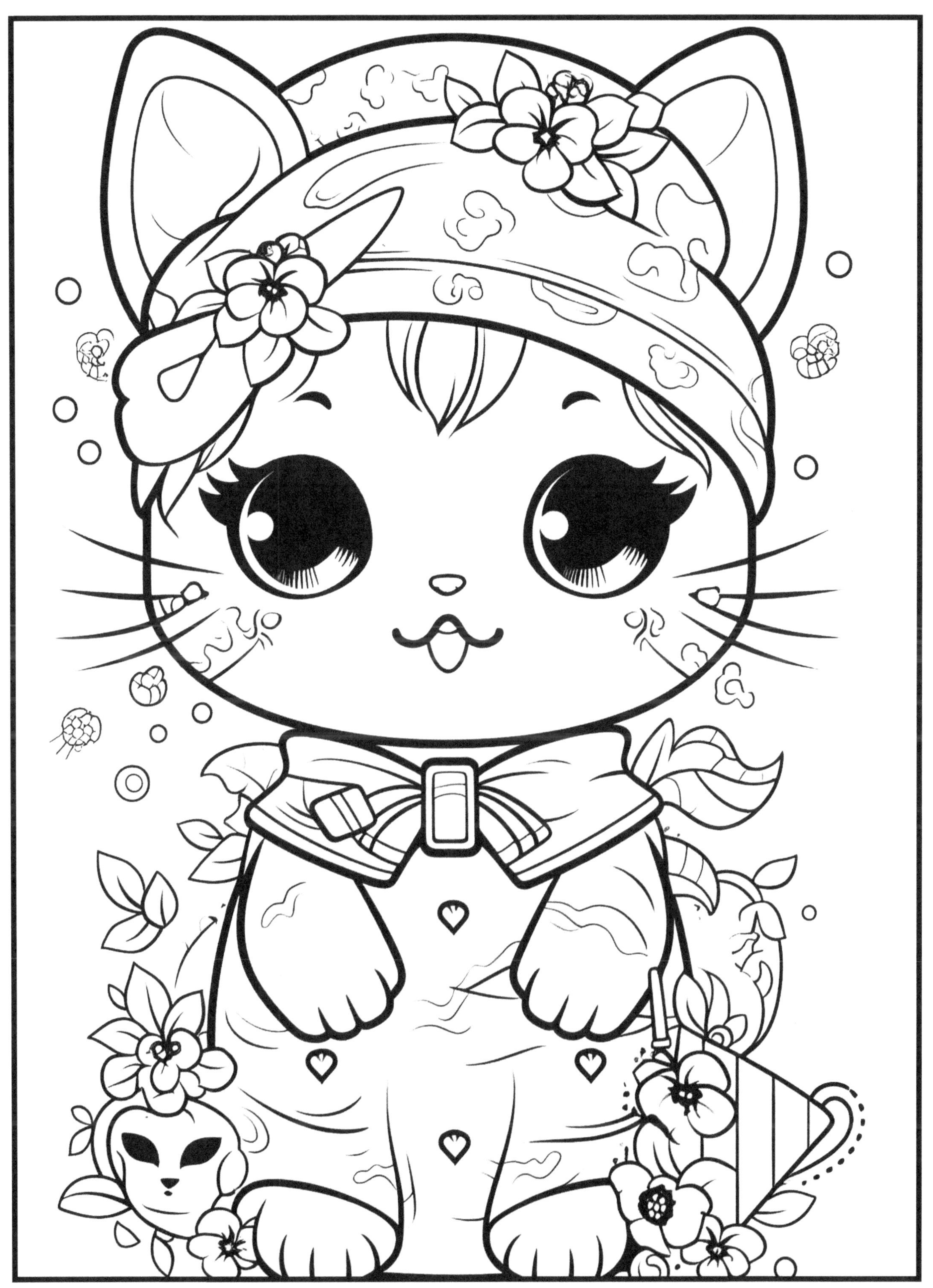

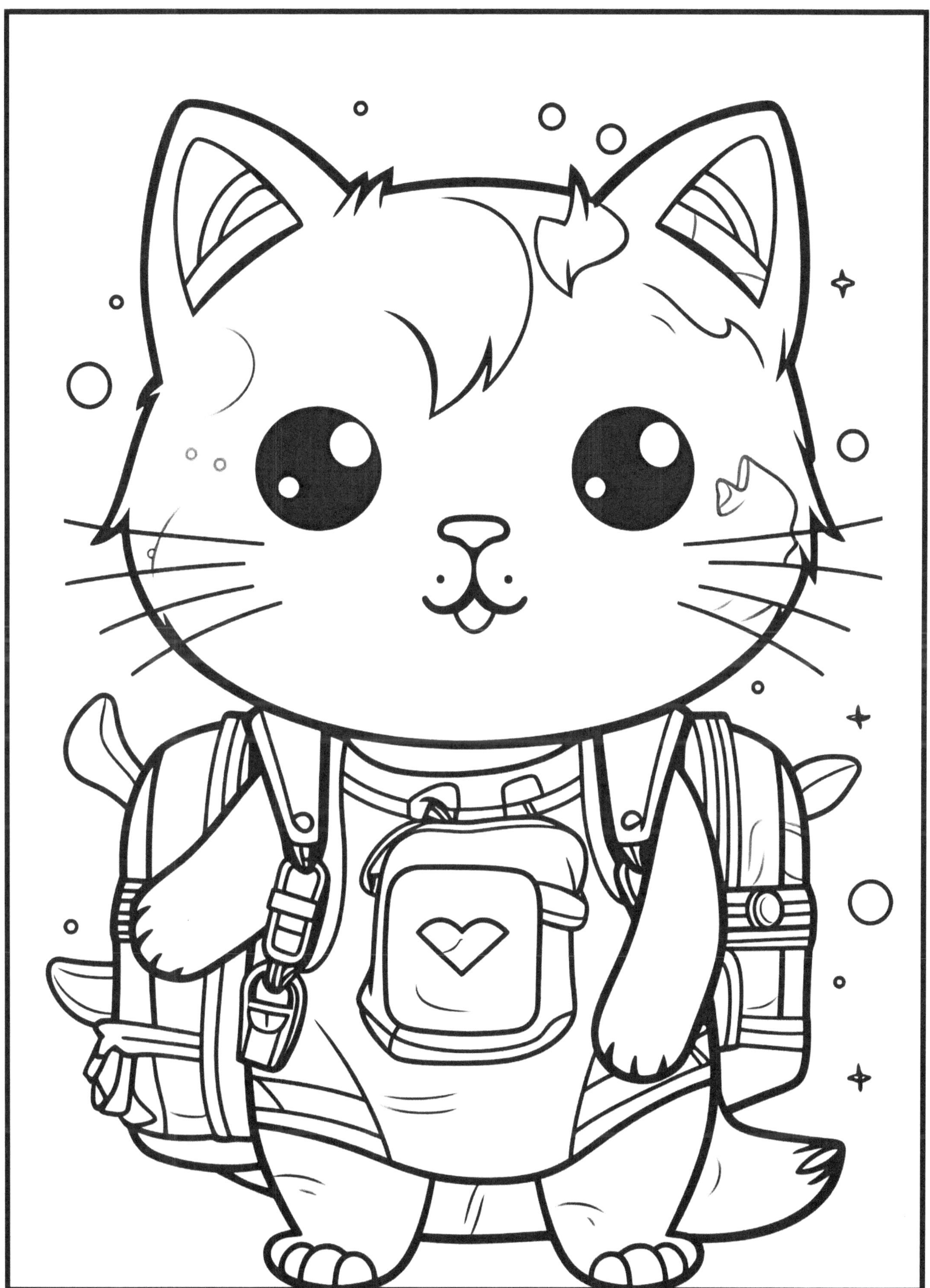

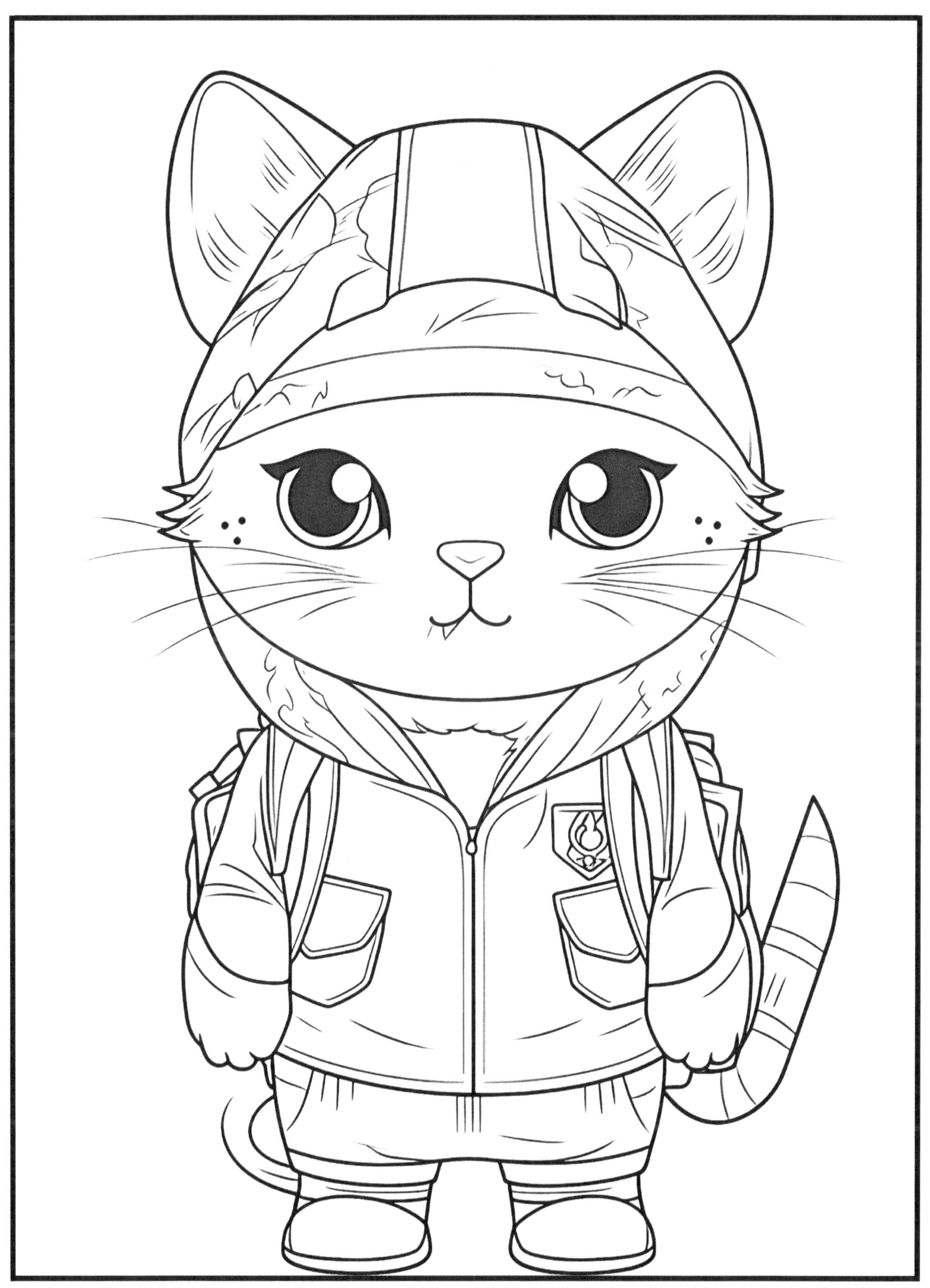

Love this Coloring book?
Want to show off your masterpiece?
Do you want your art displayed on our site?

No registration required

1.   Take a picture of a finished coloring page
2.   Scan the QR Code to go to our website
3.   Upload the photo of your finished coloring page

OR

Use #happytimesbooks or mention us
@happytimesbooks on Instragram to have it
displayed on our front page

If you are under 18 years old, please get a parents permission

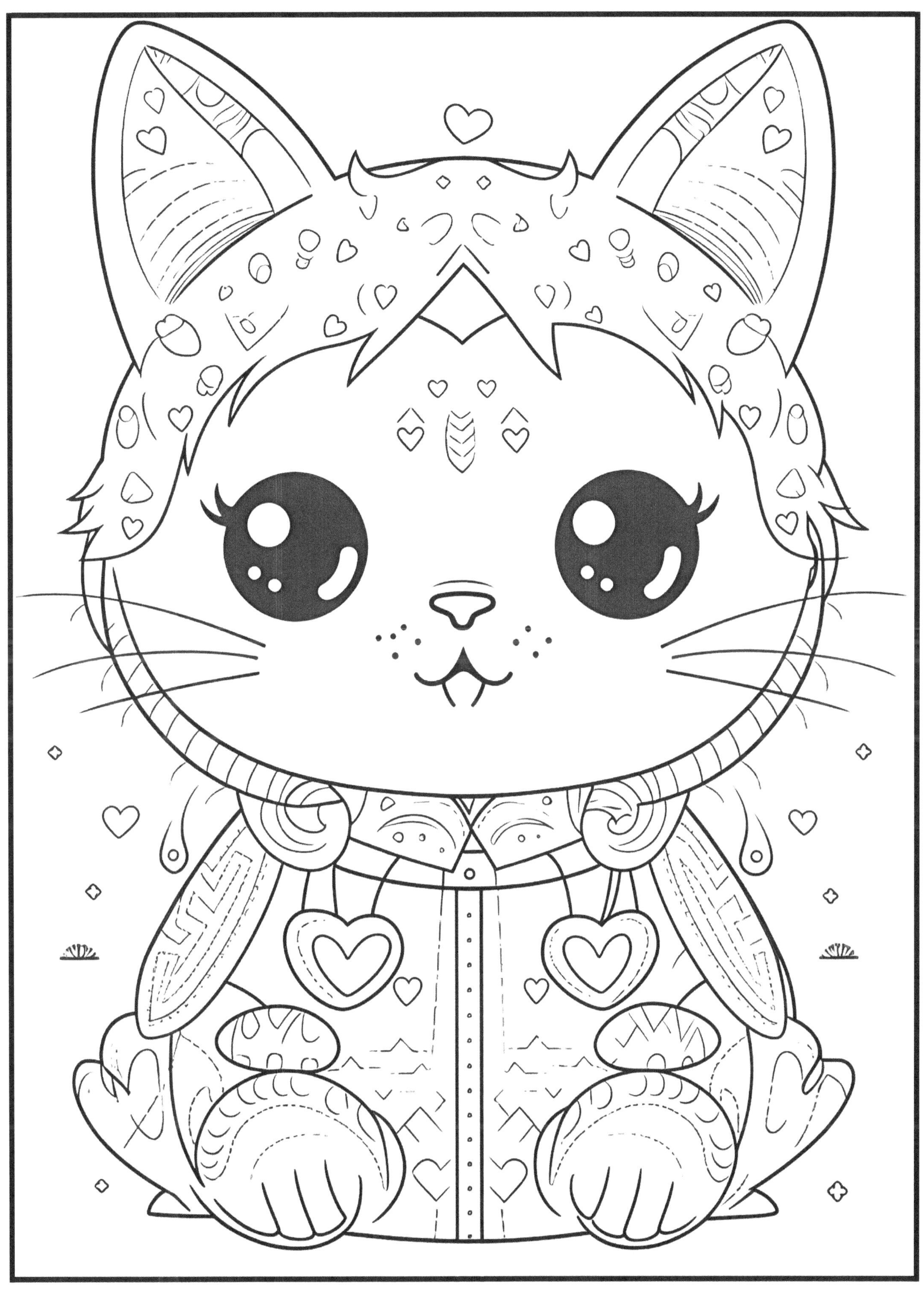

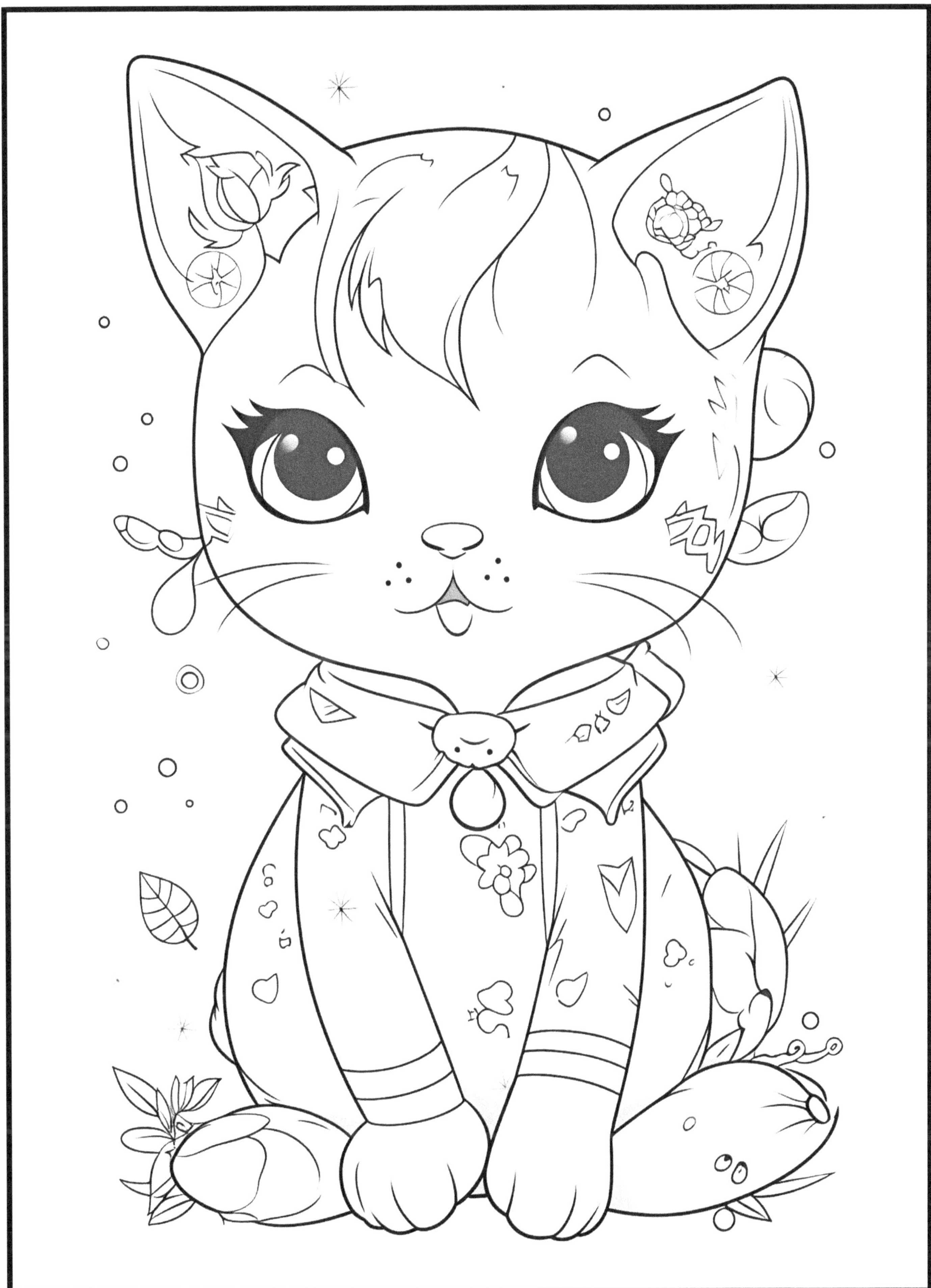

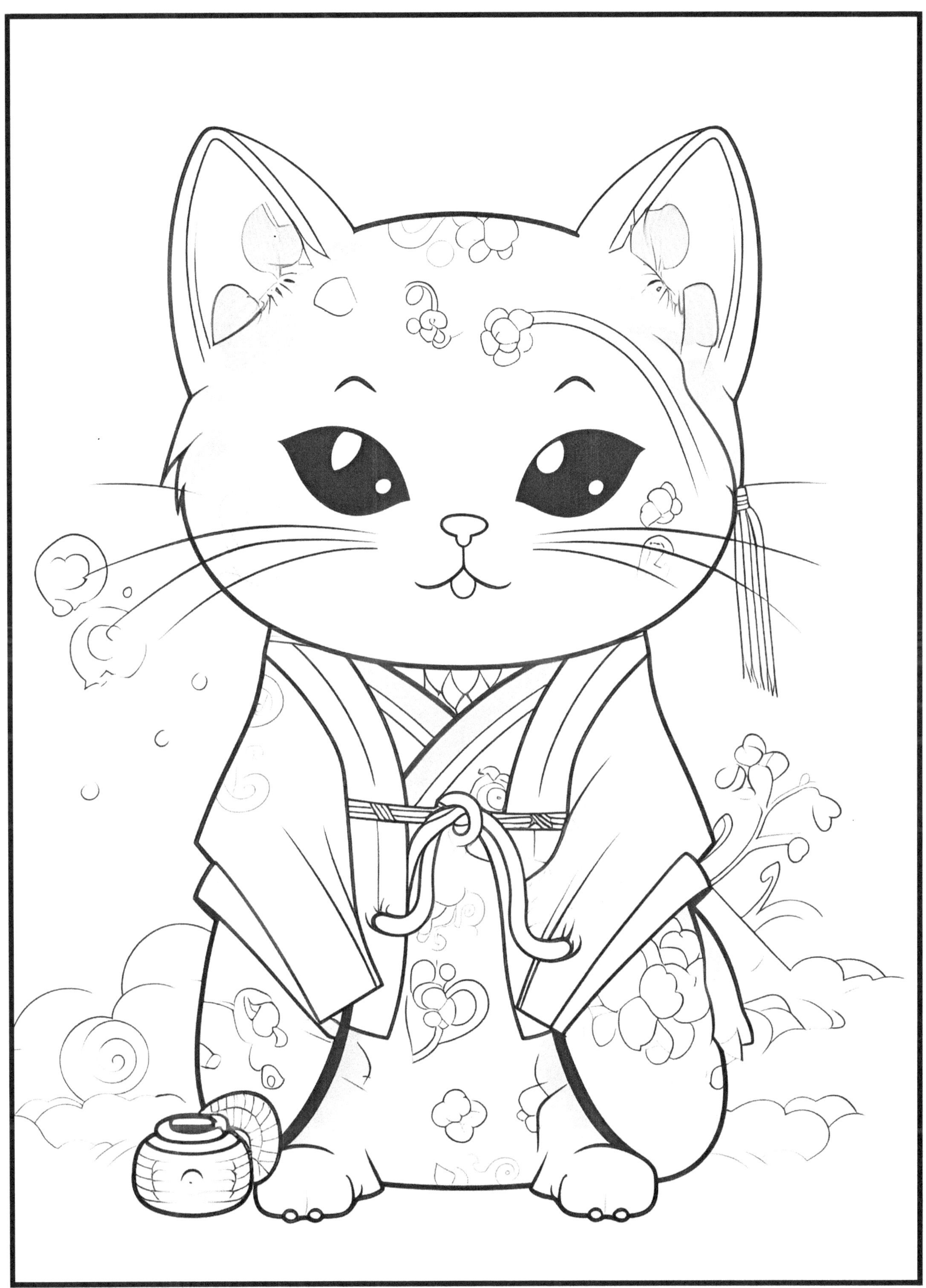

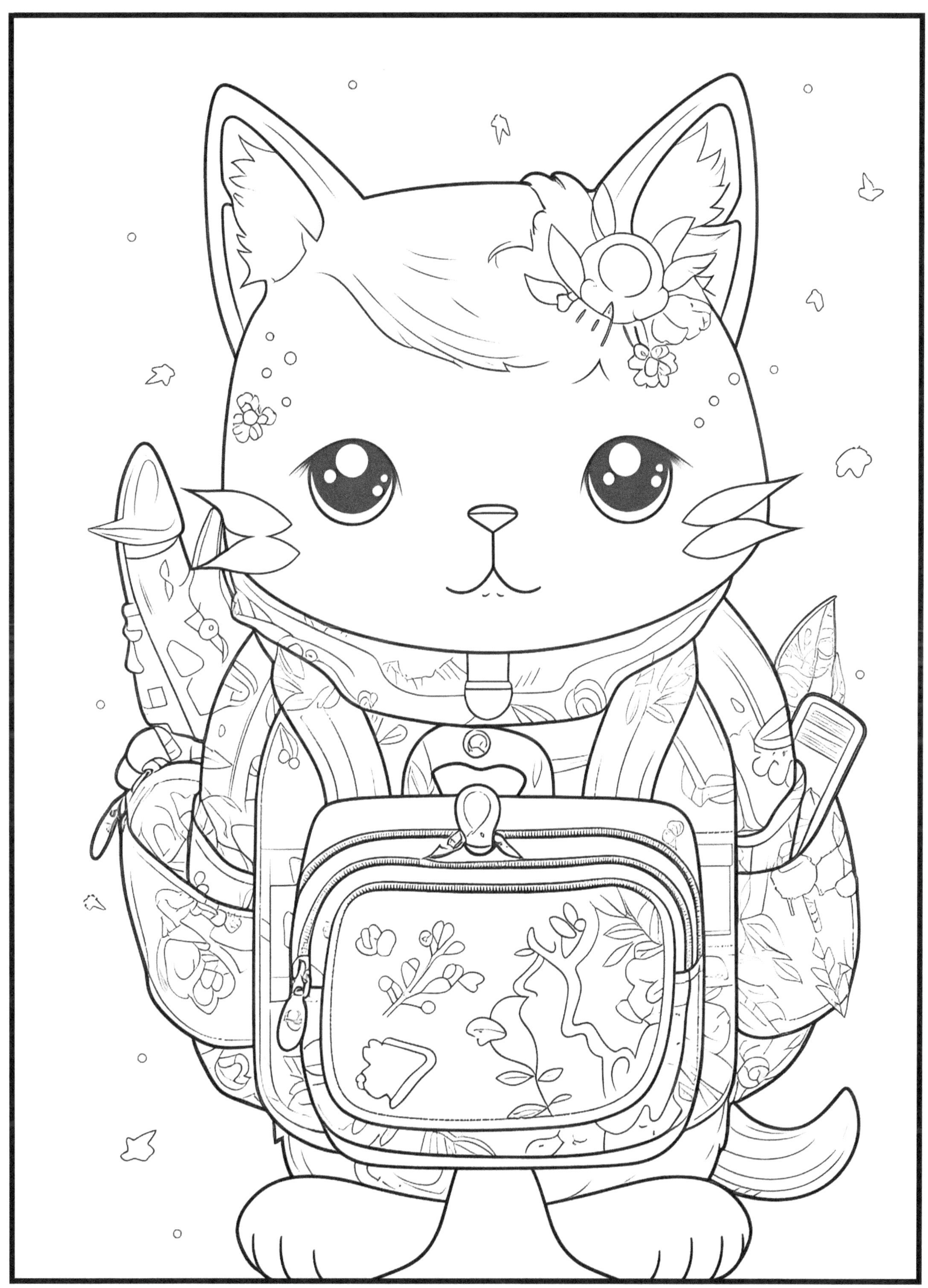

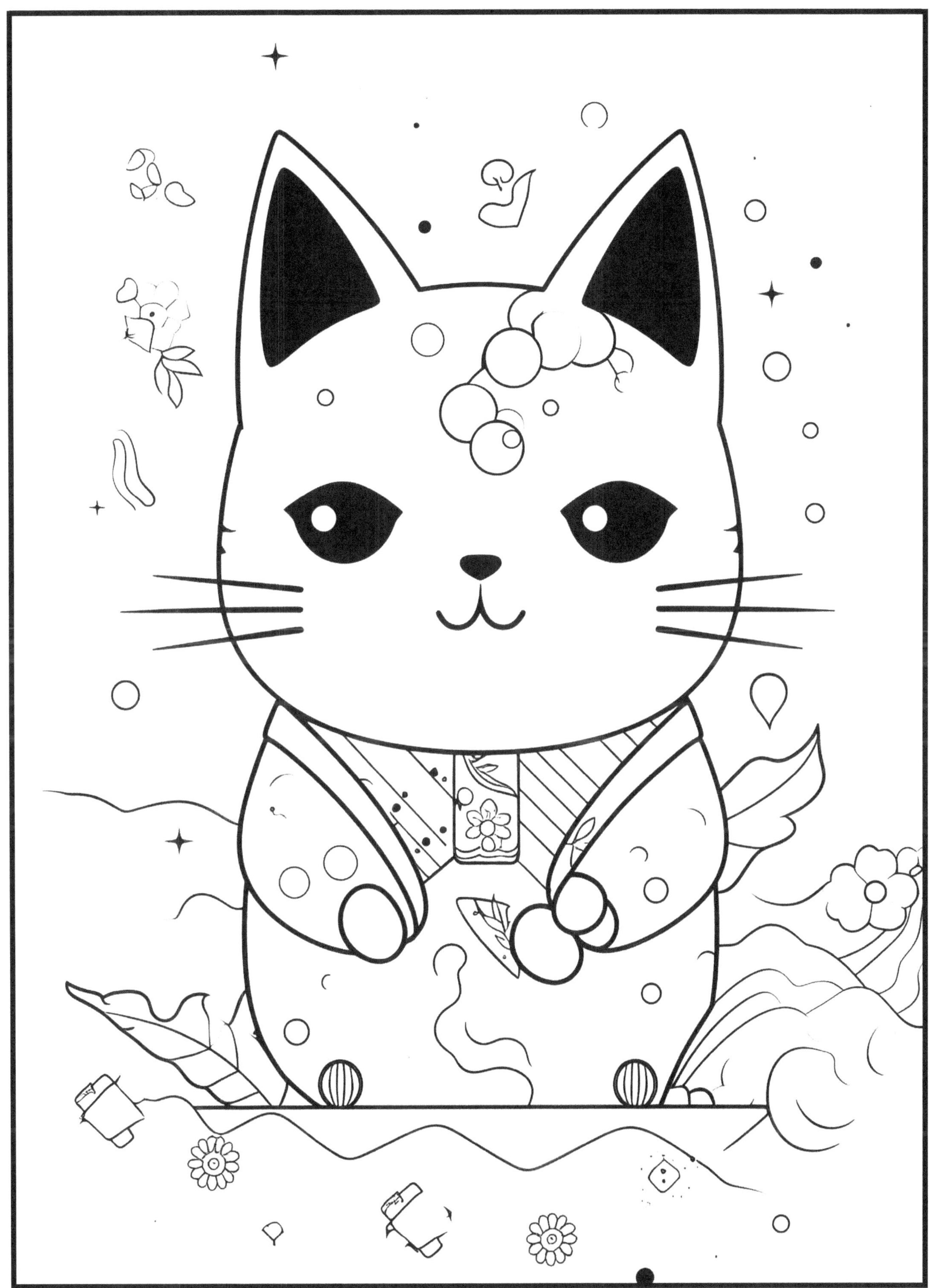

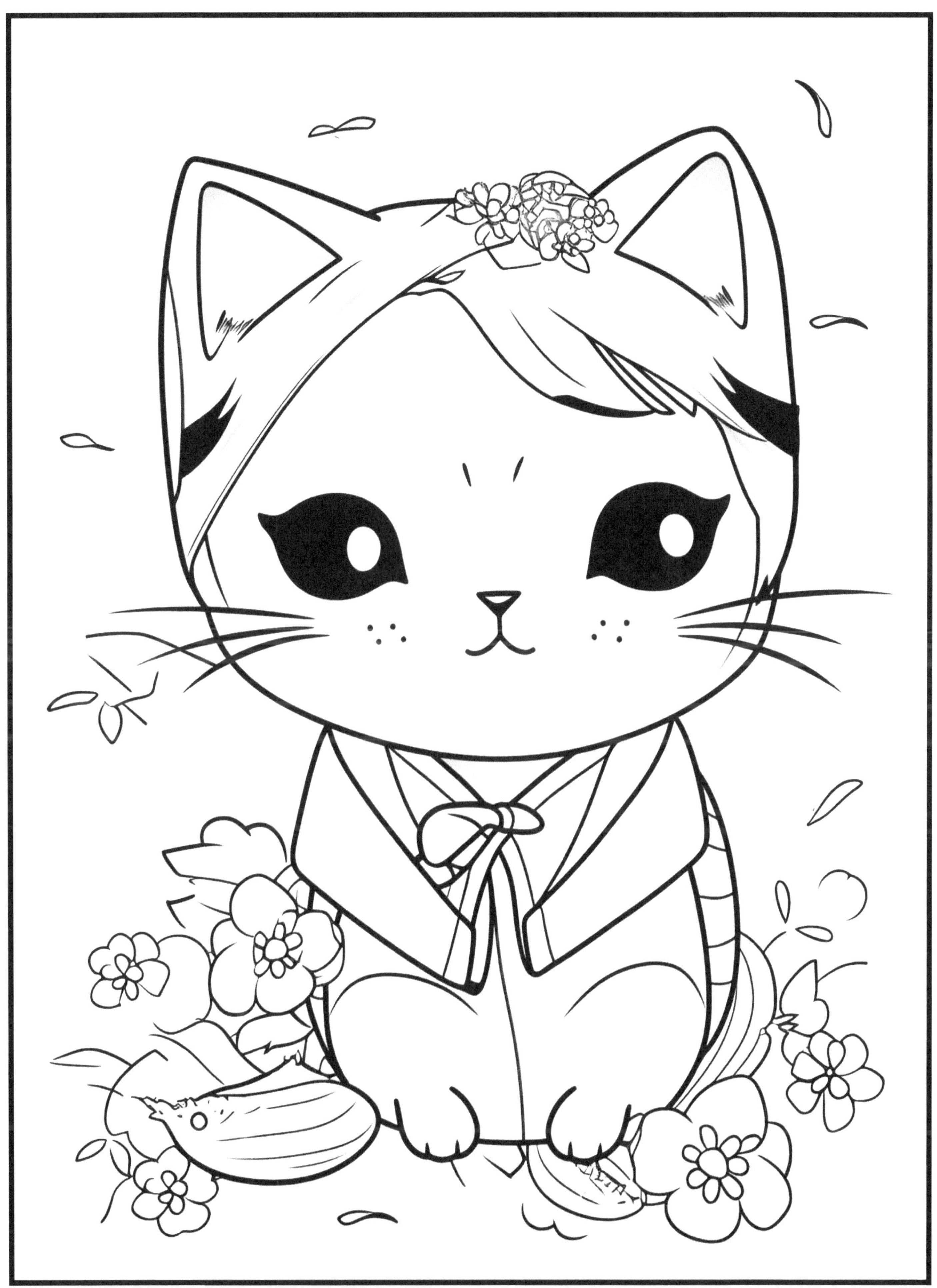

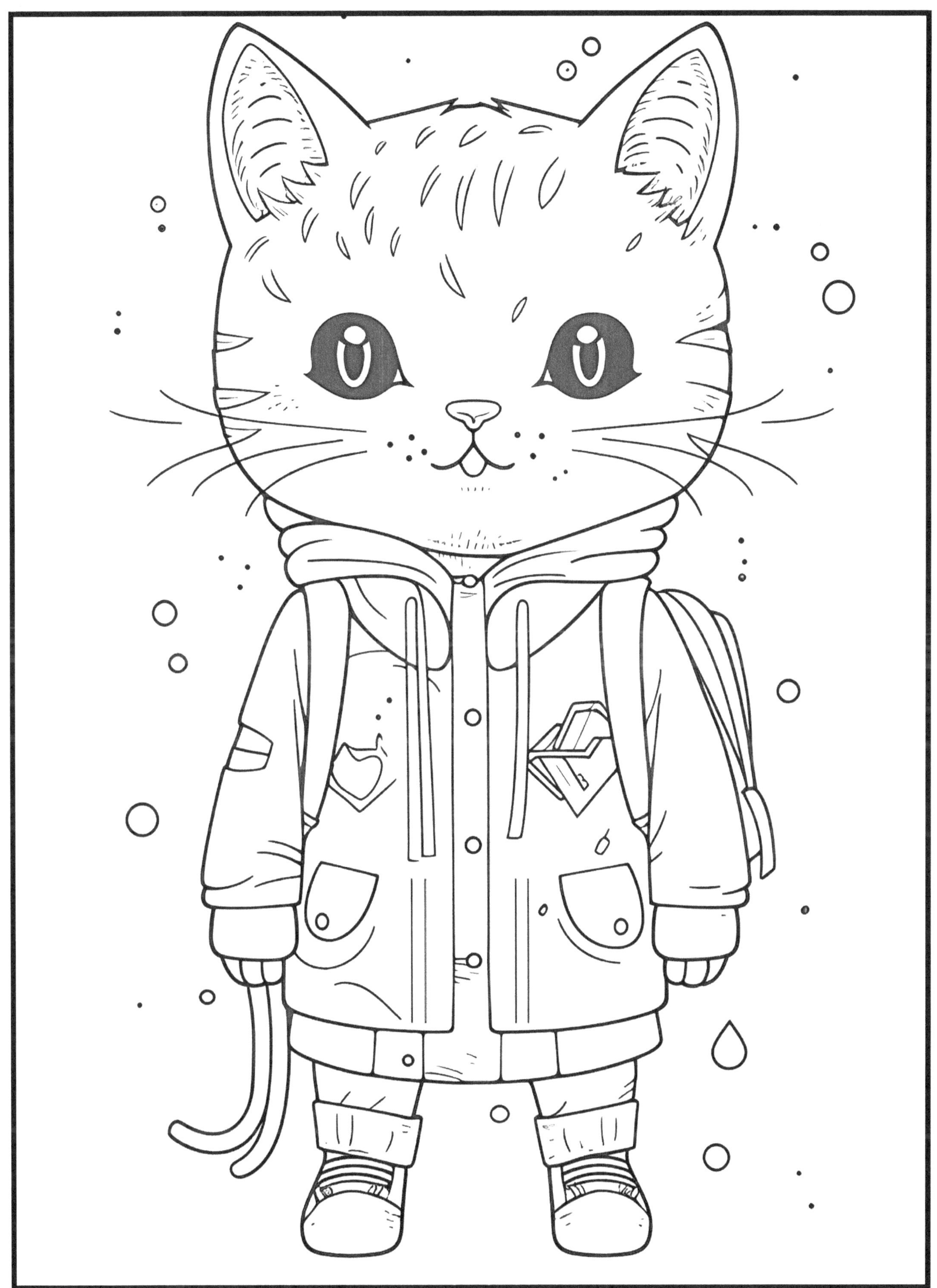

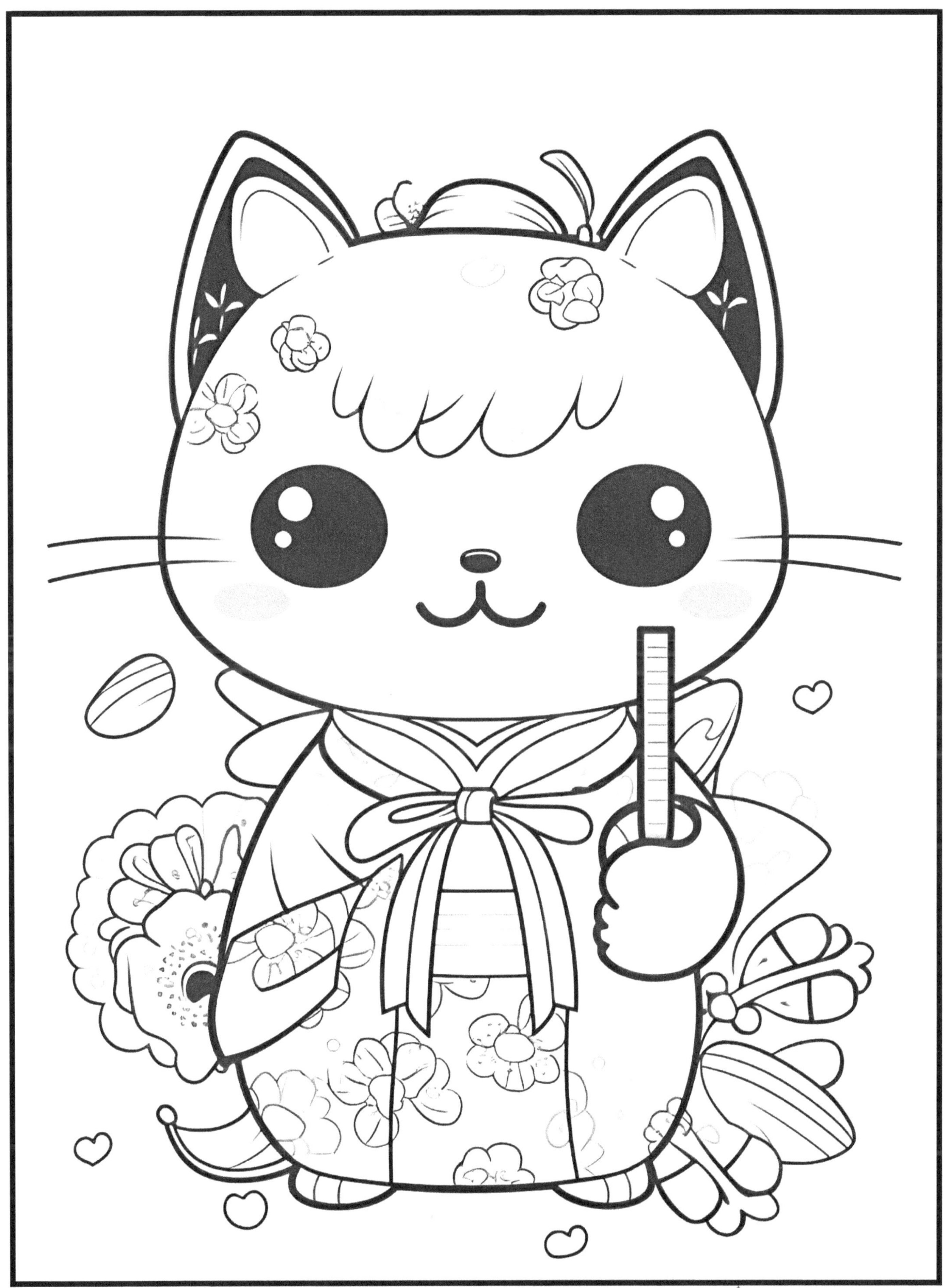

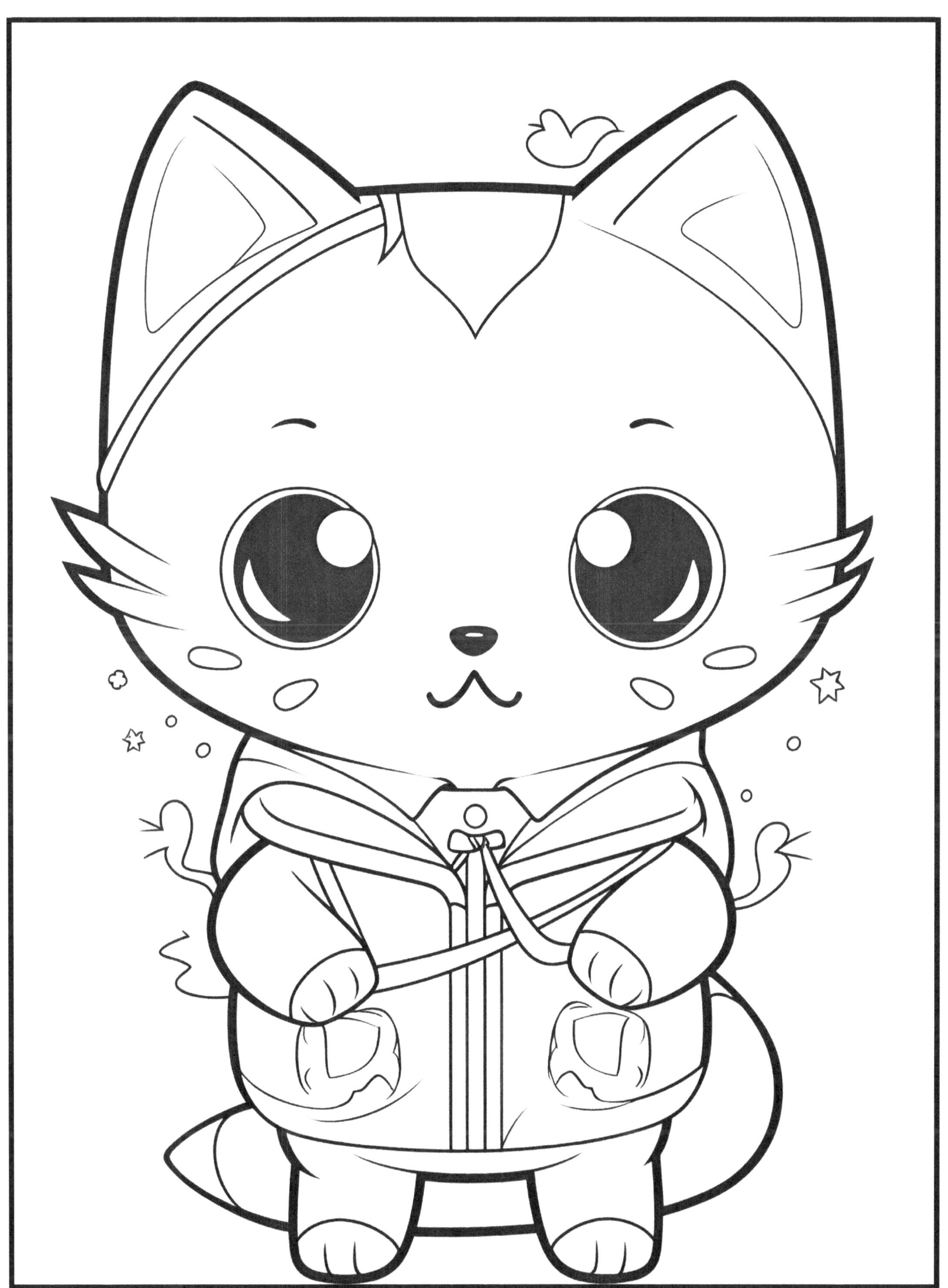

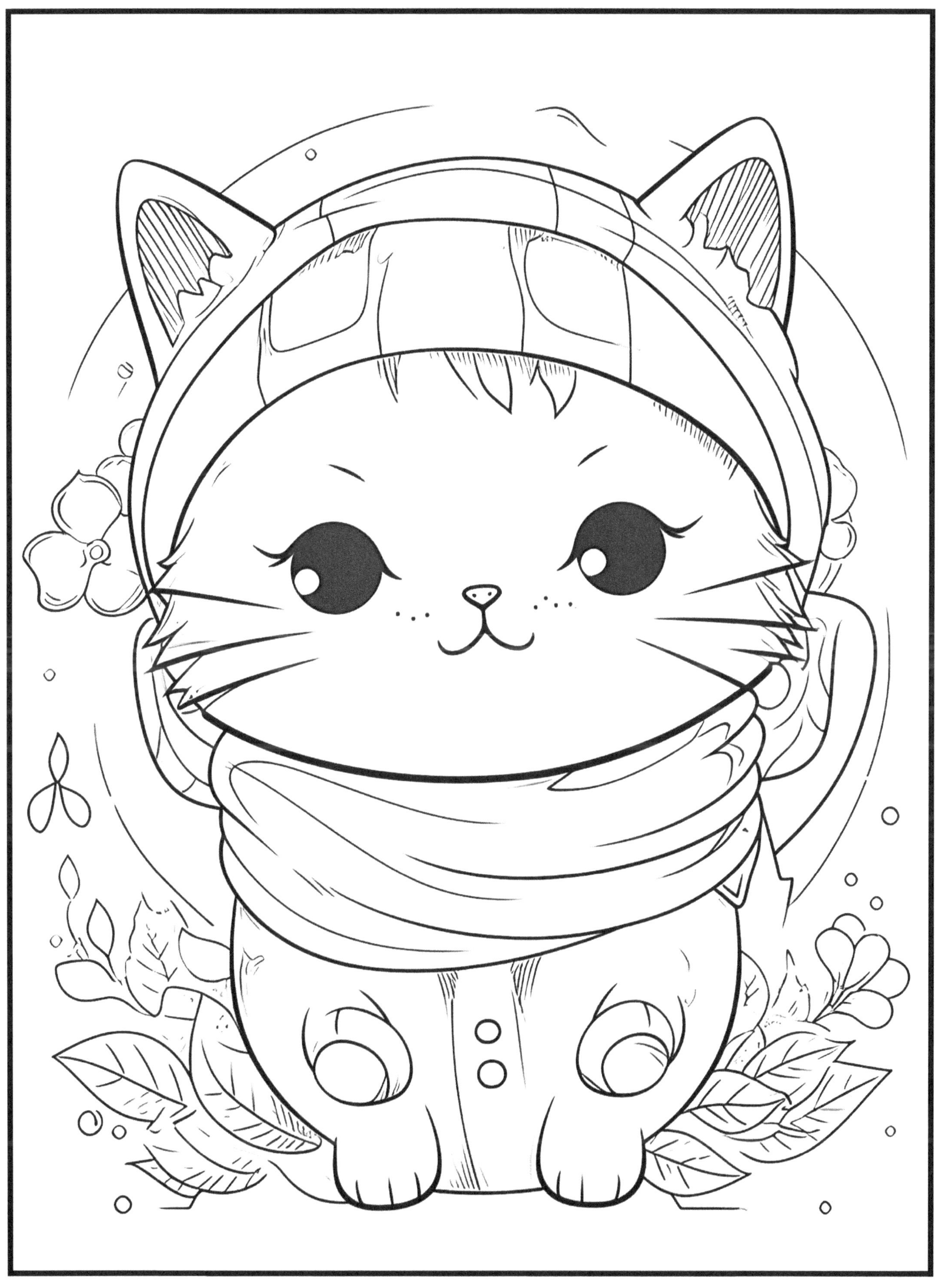

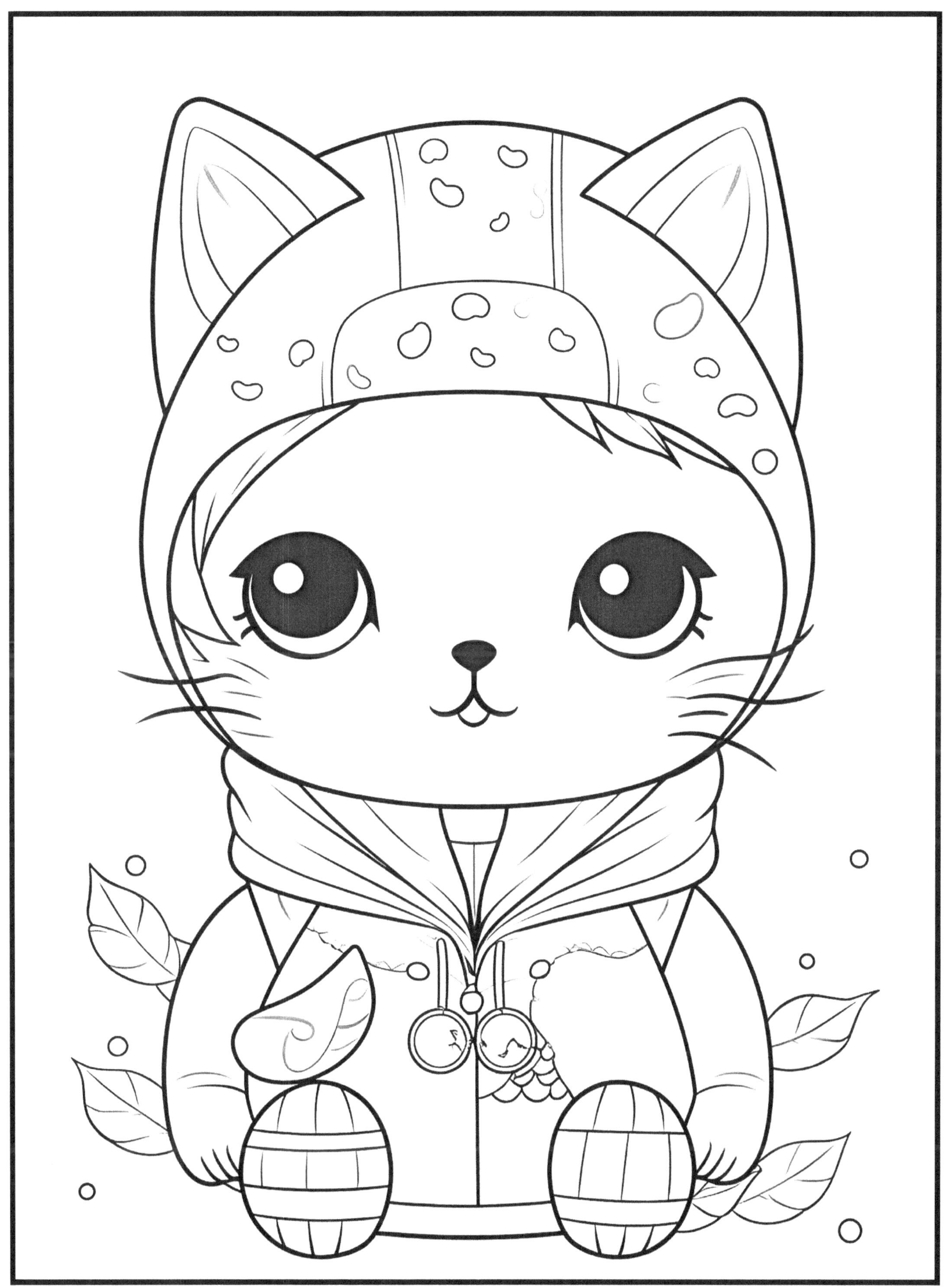

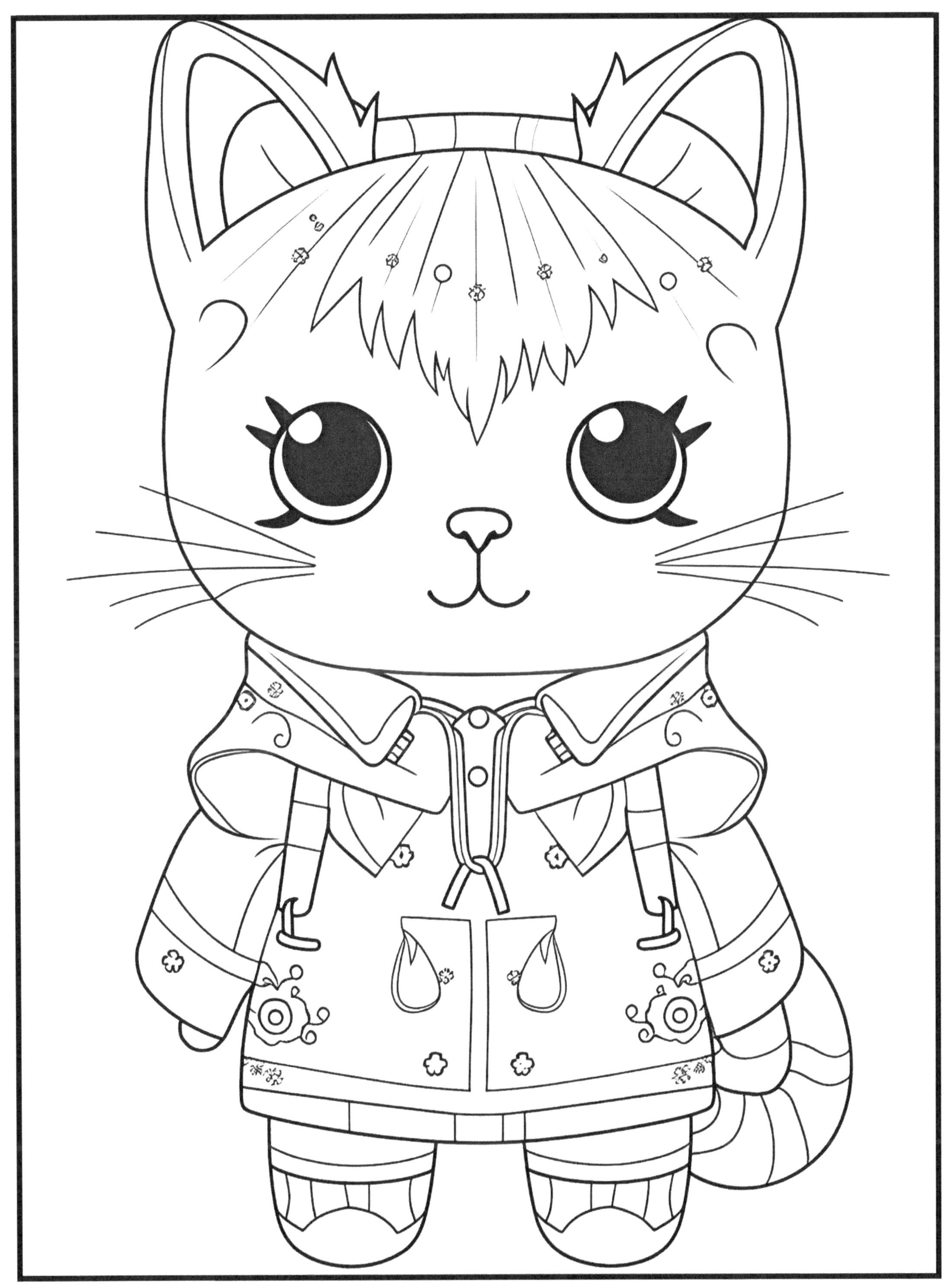

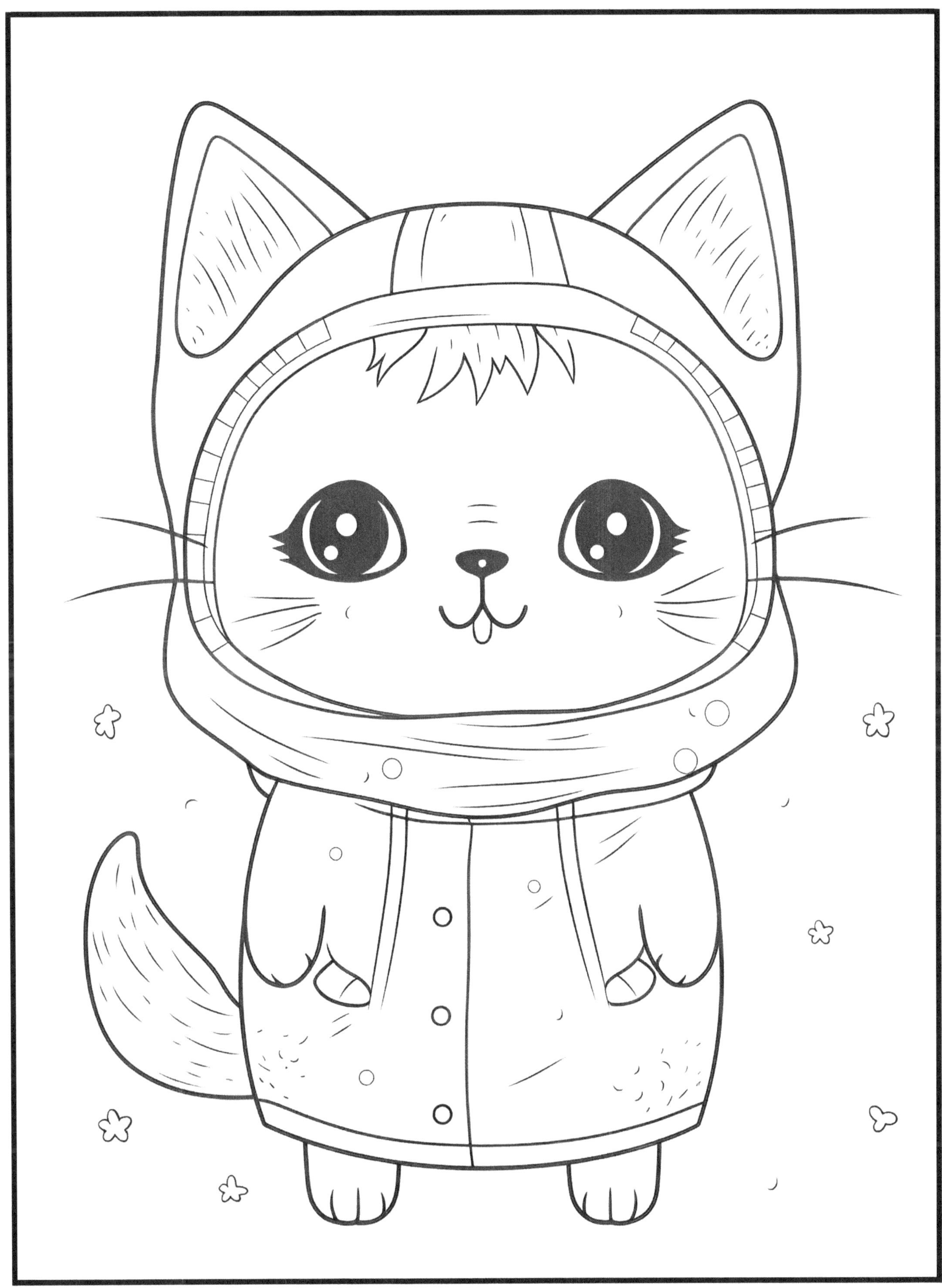

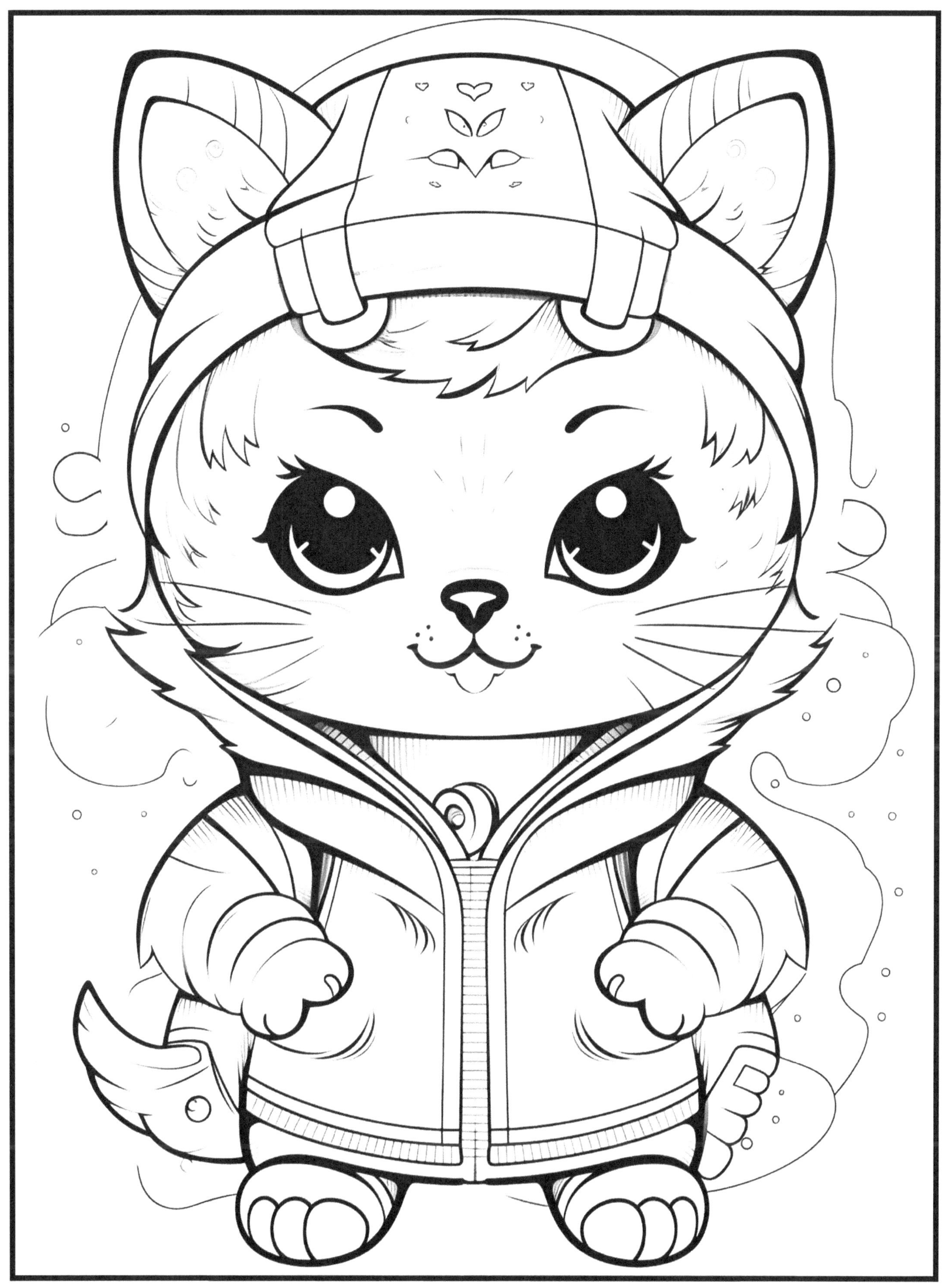

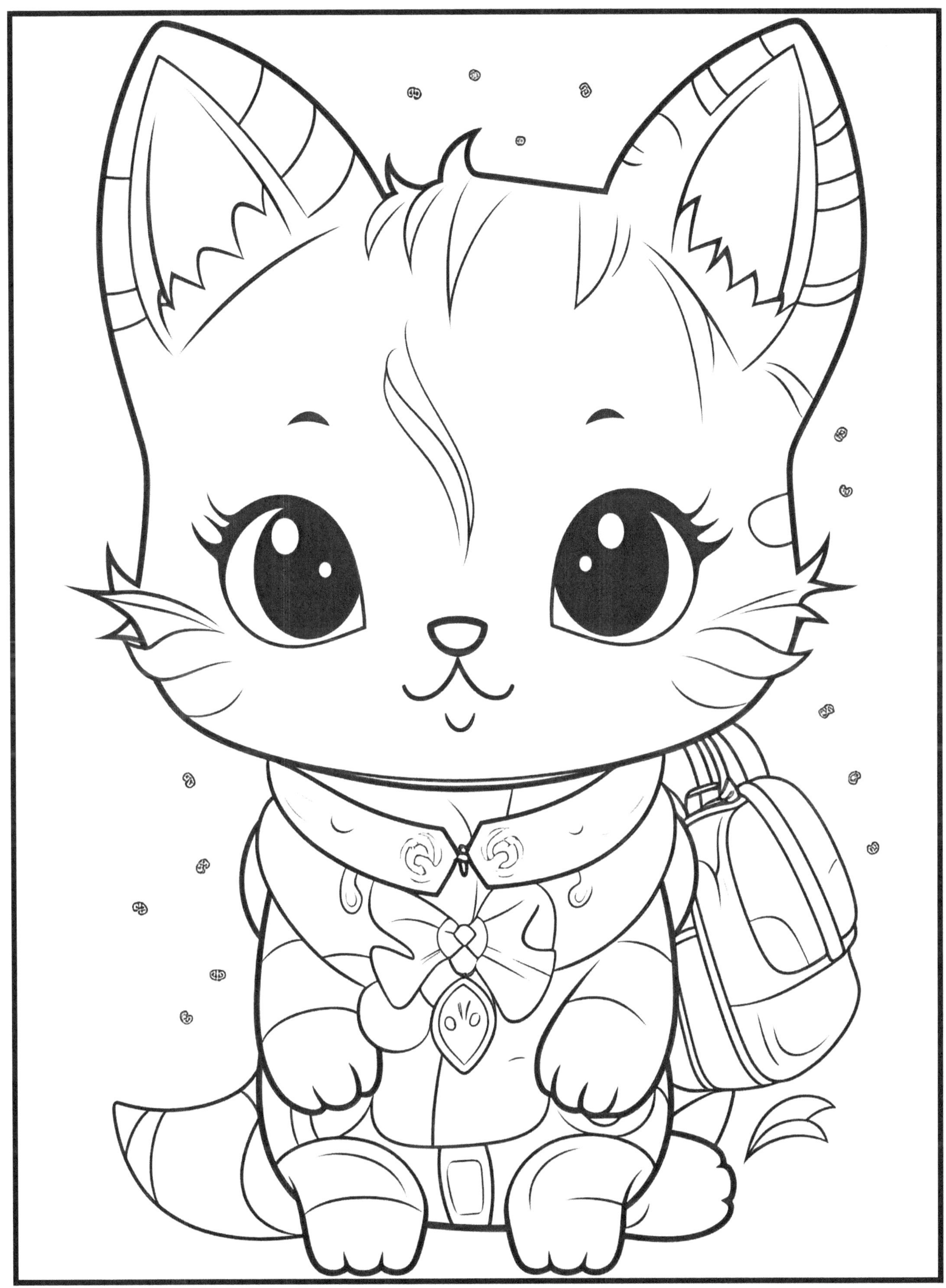

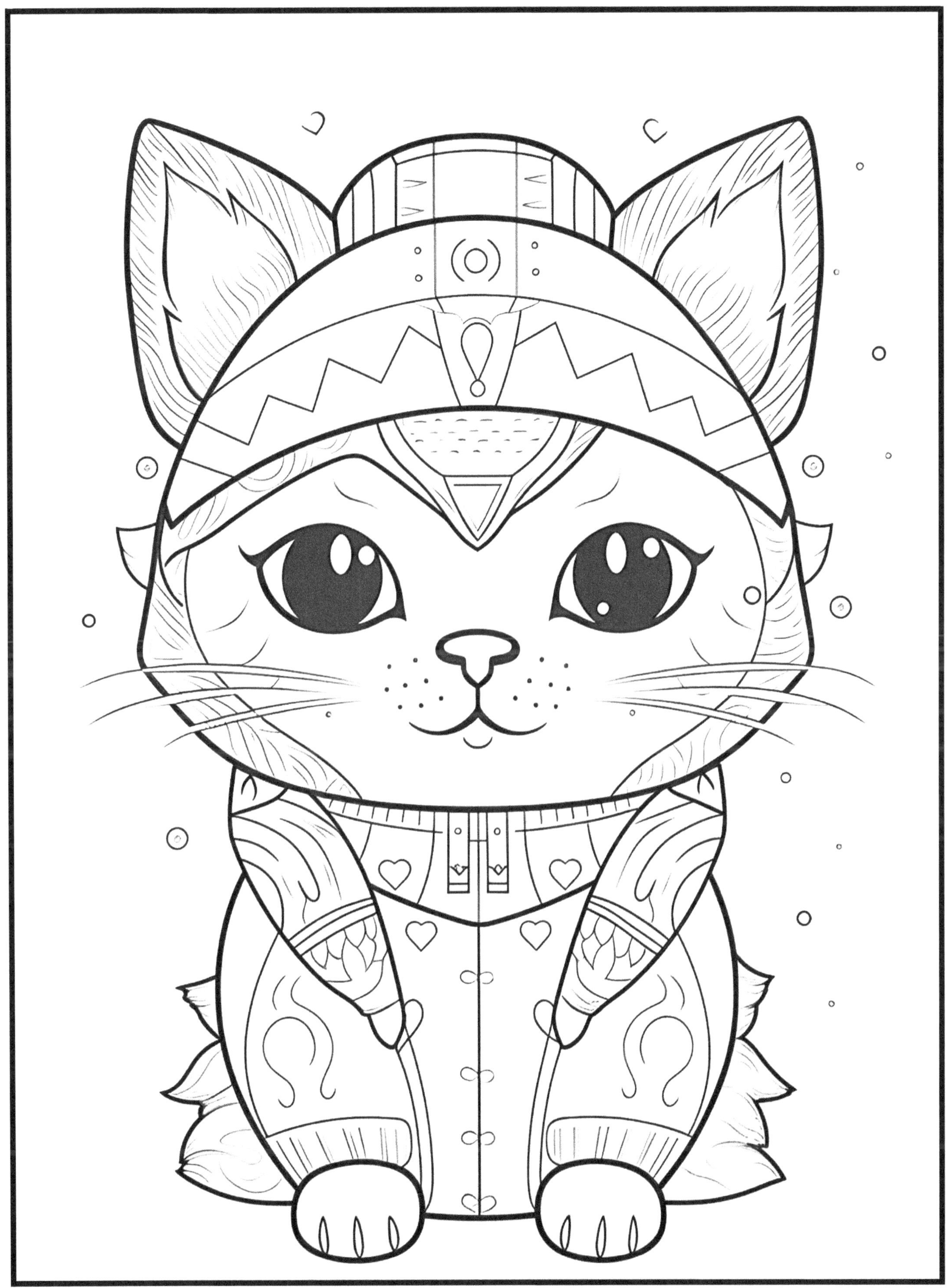

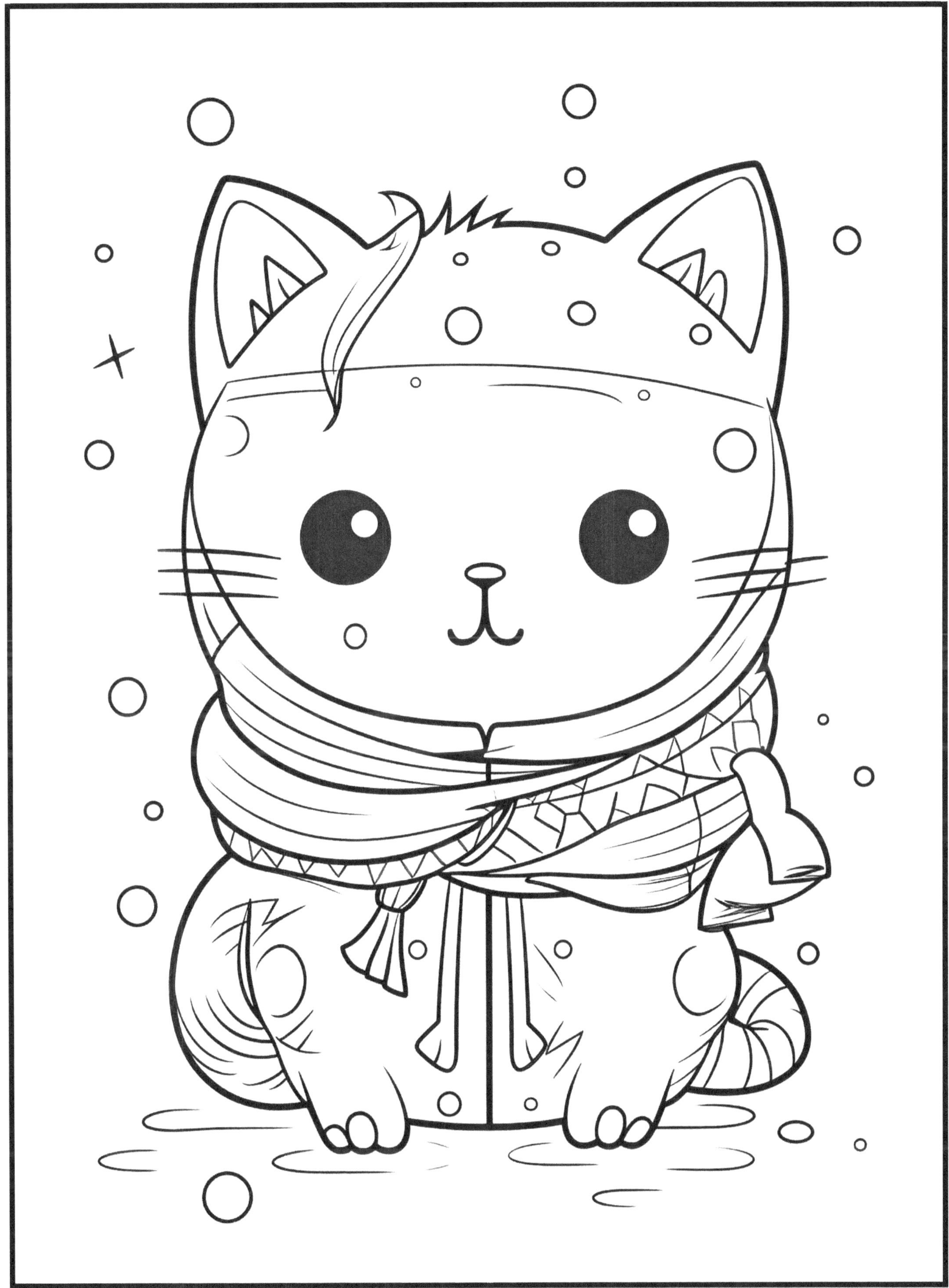

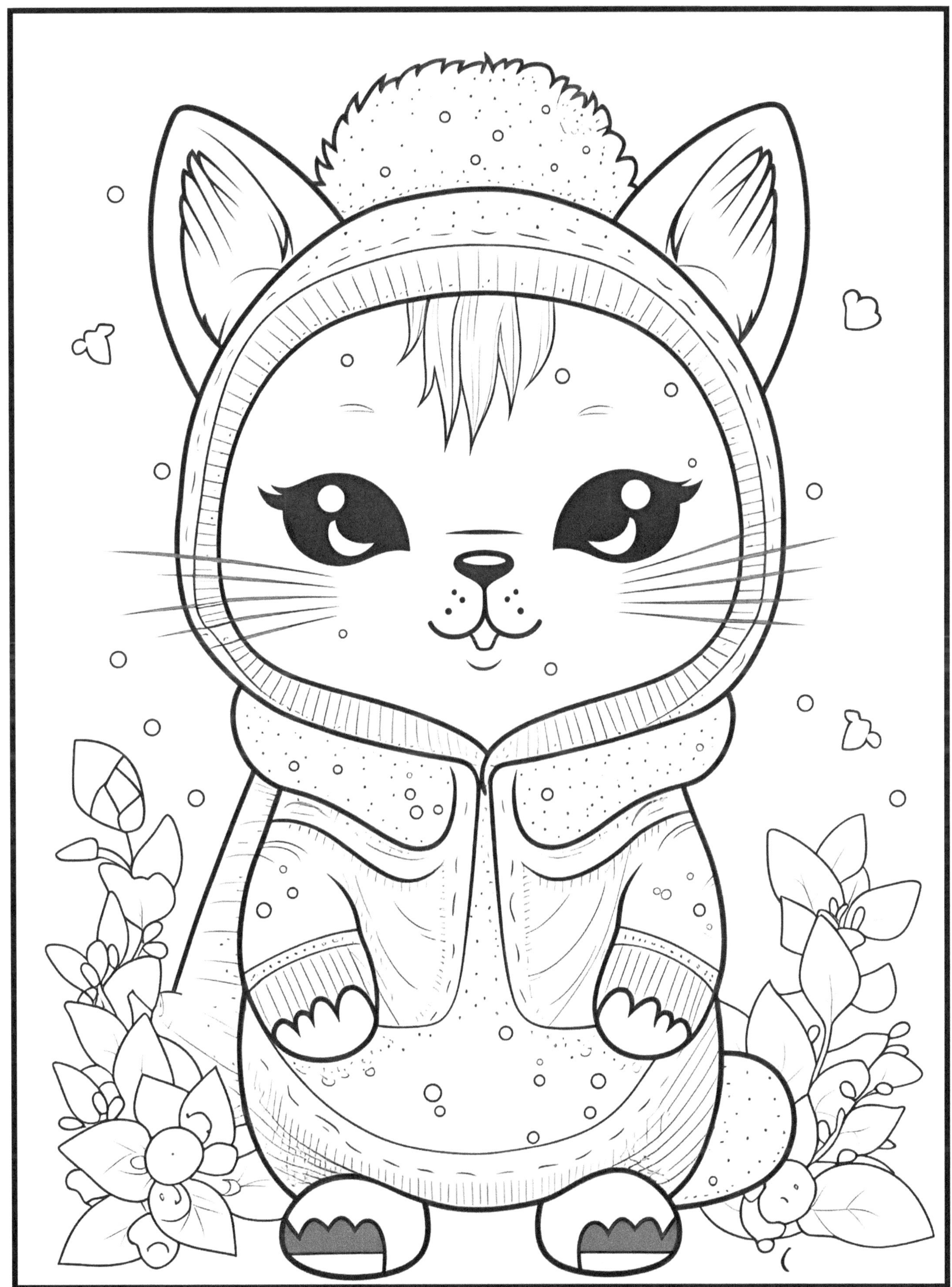

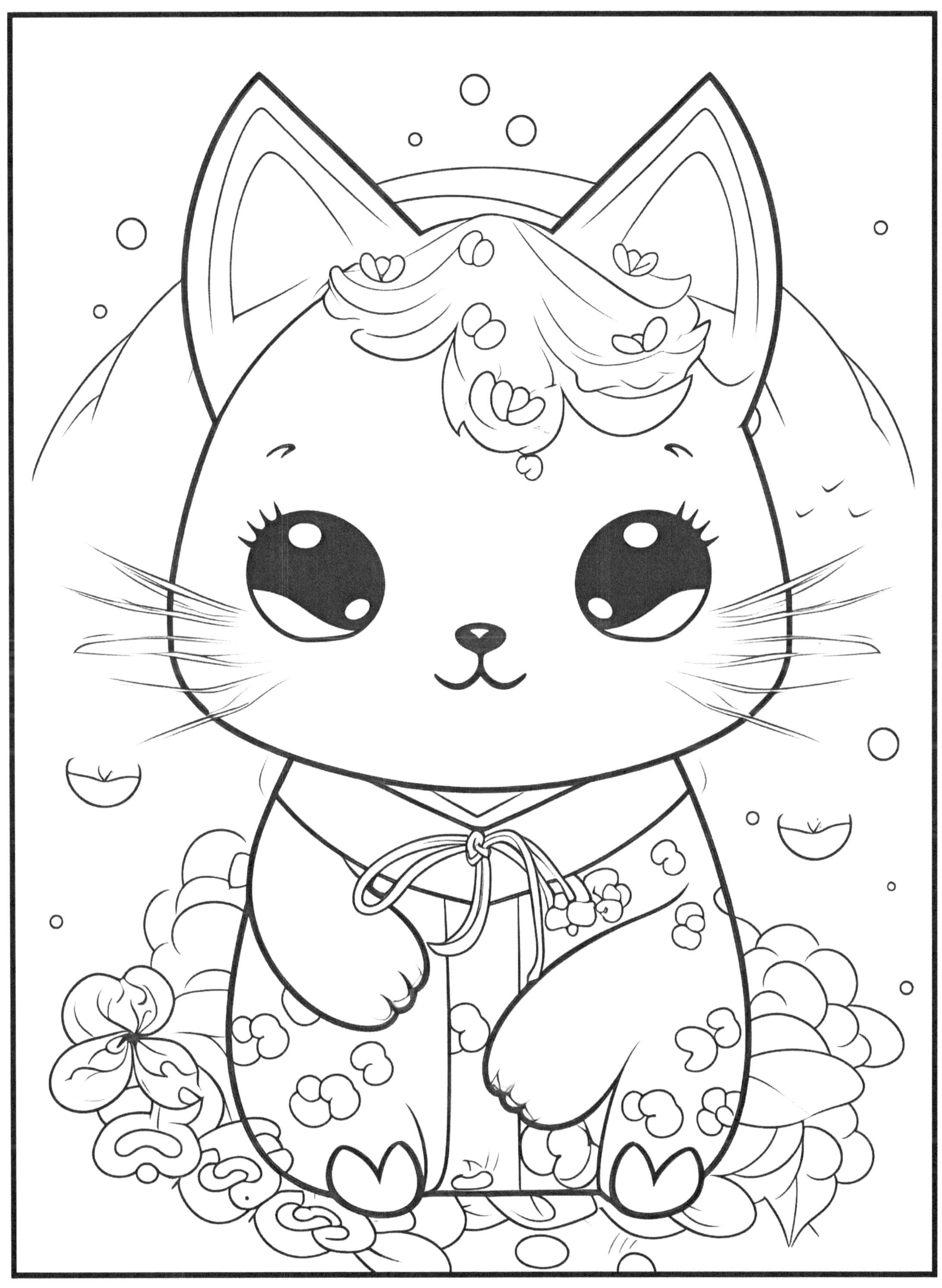

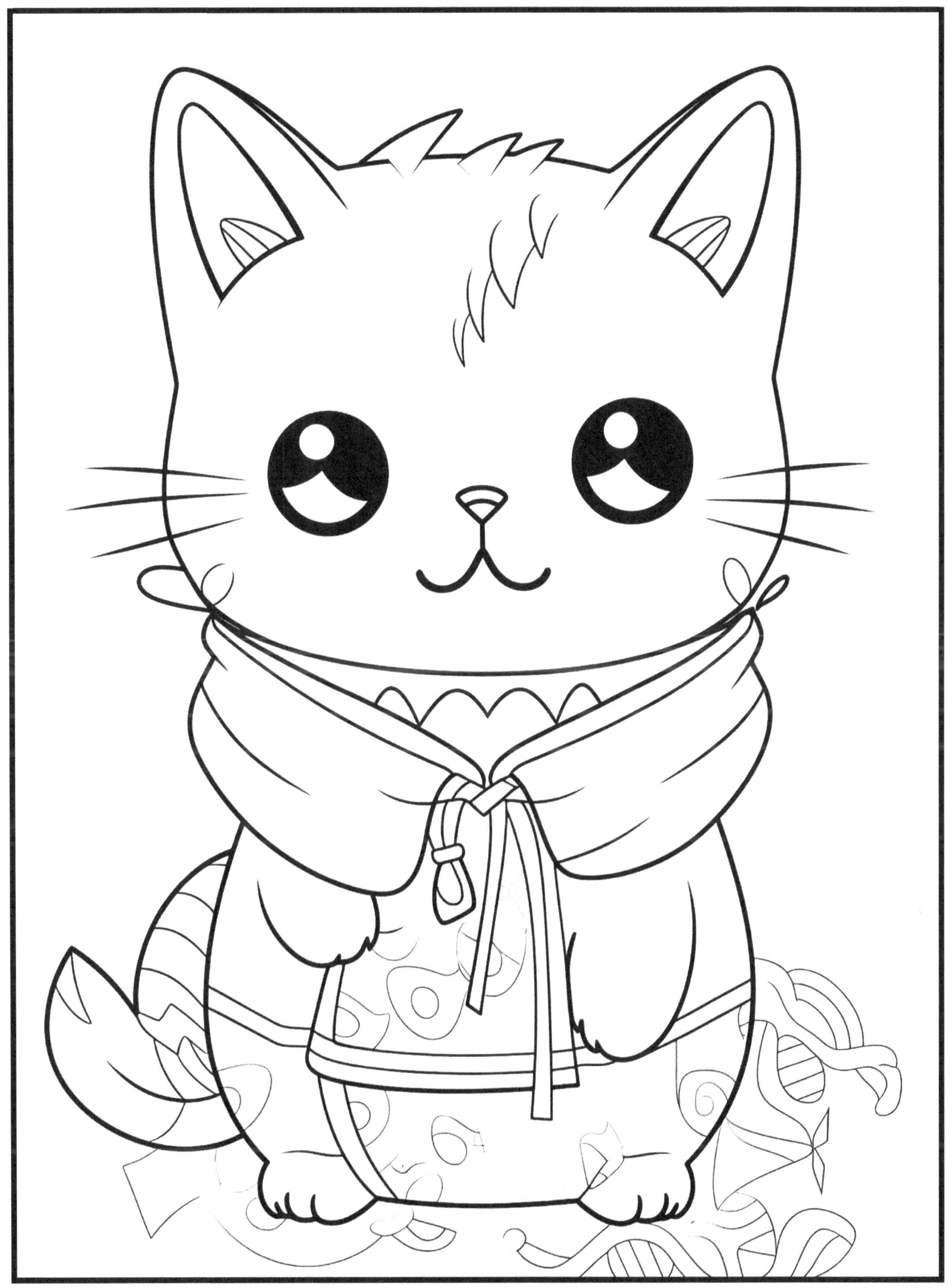

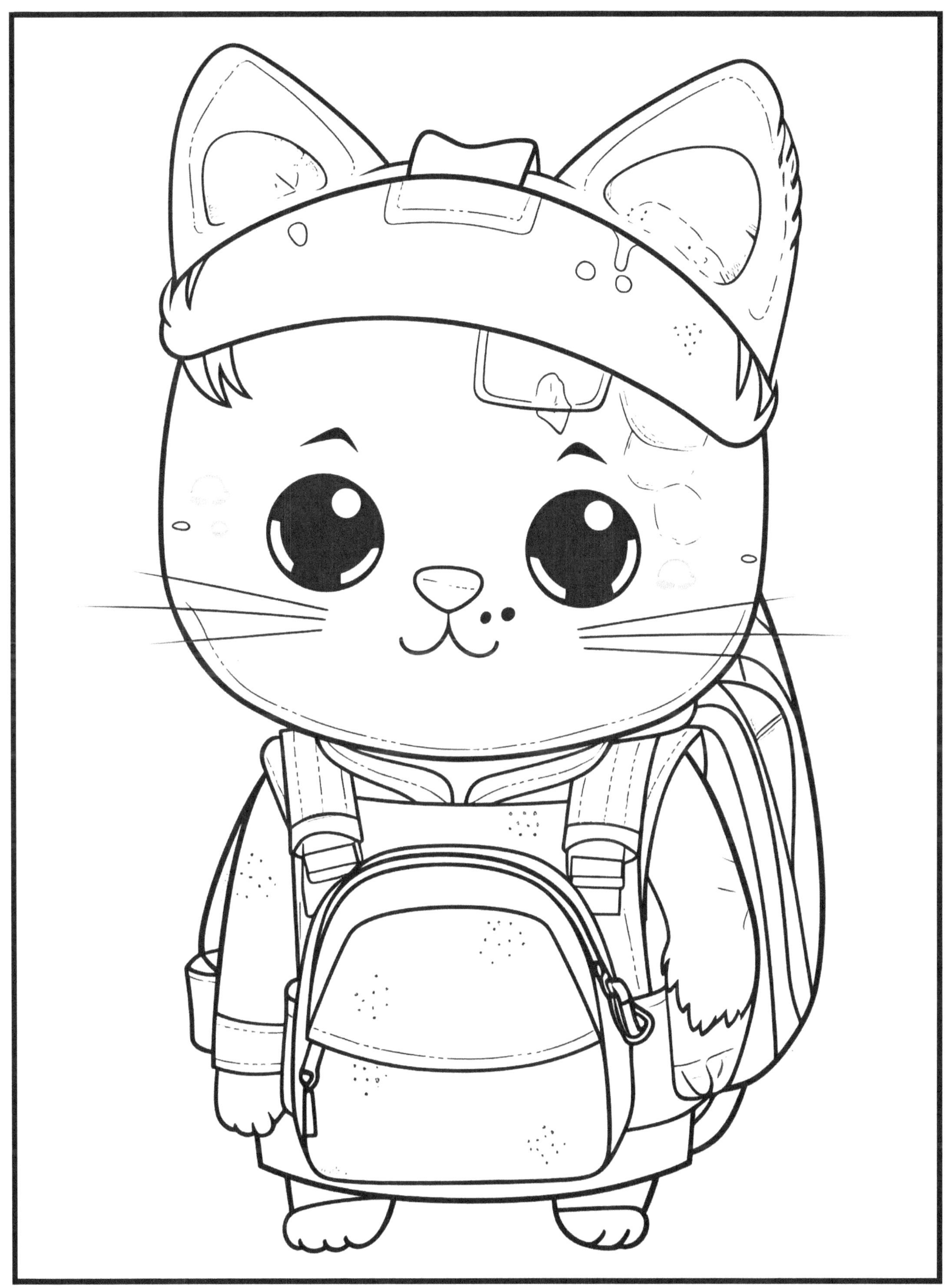

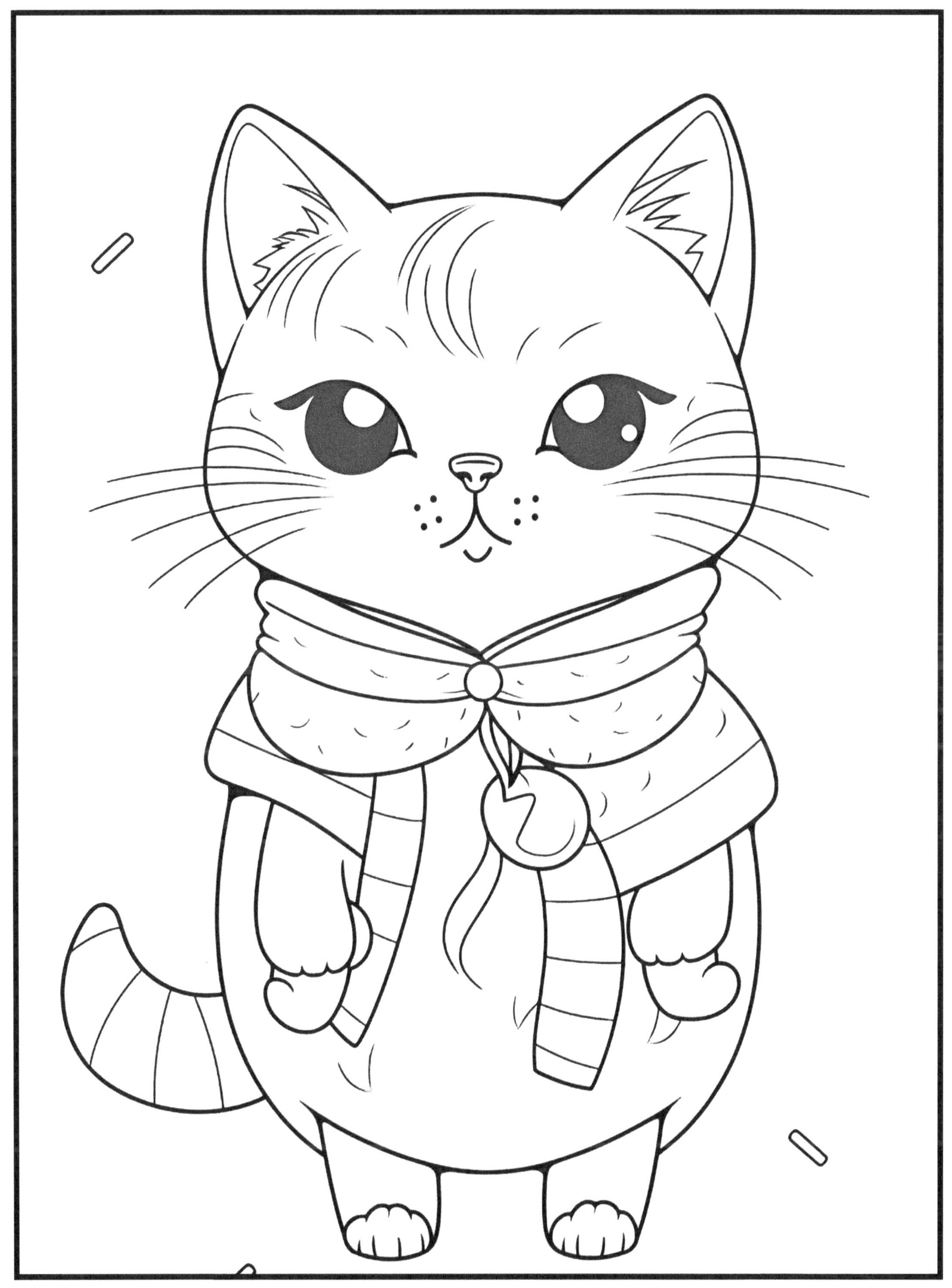

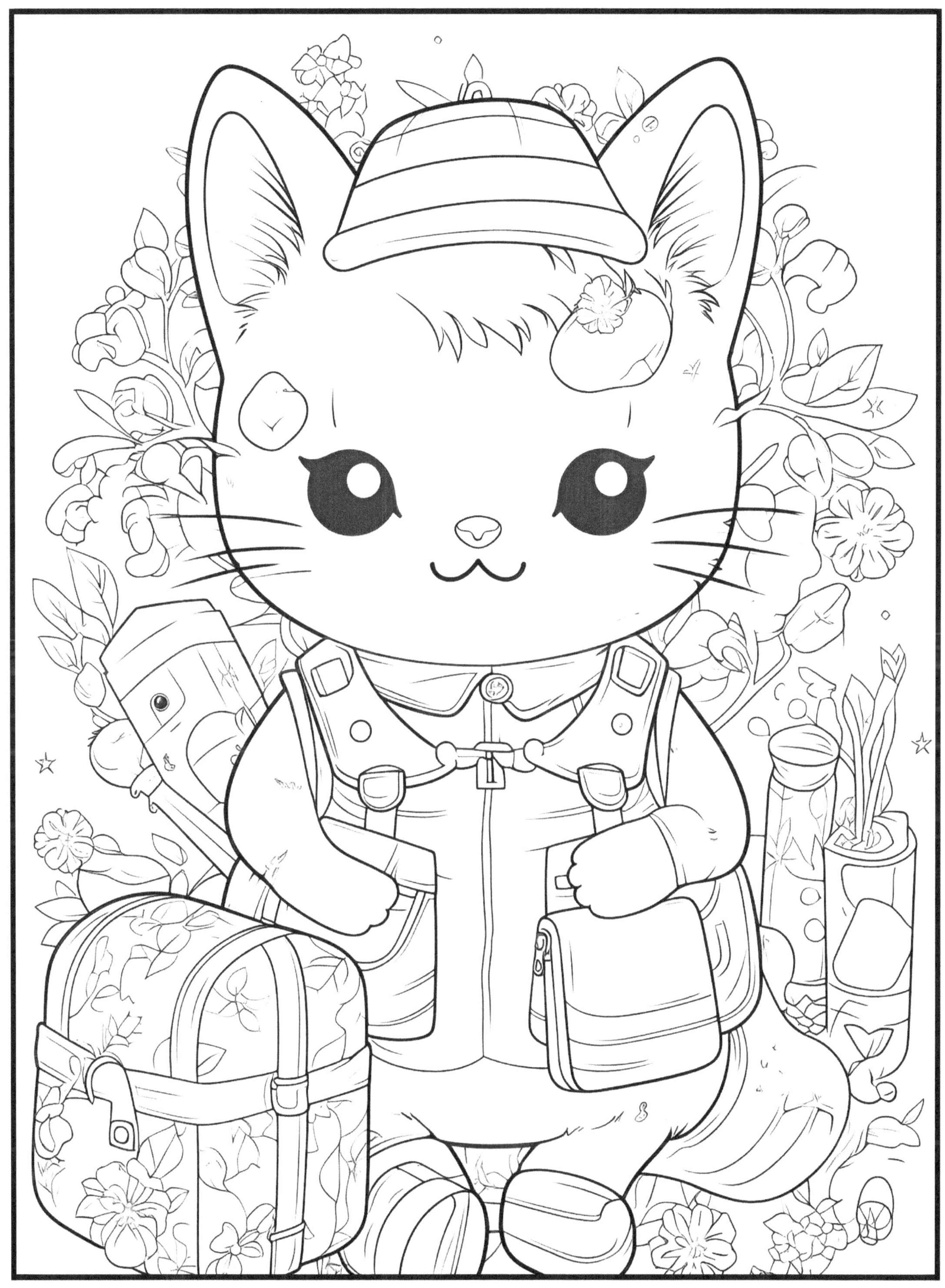

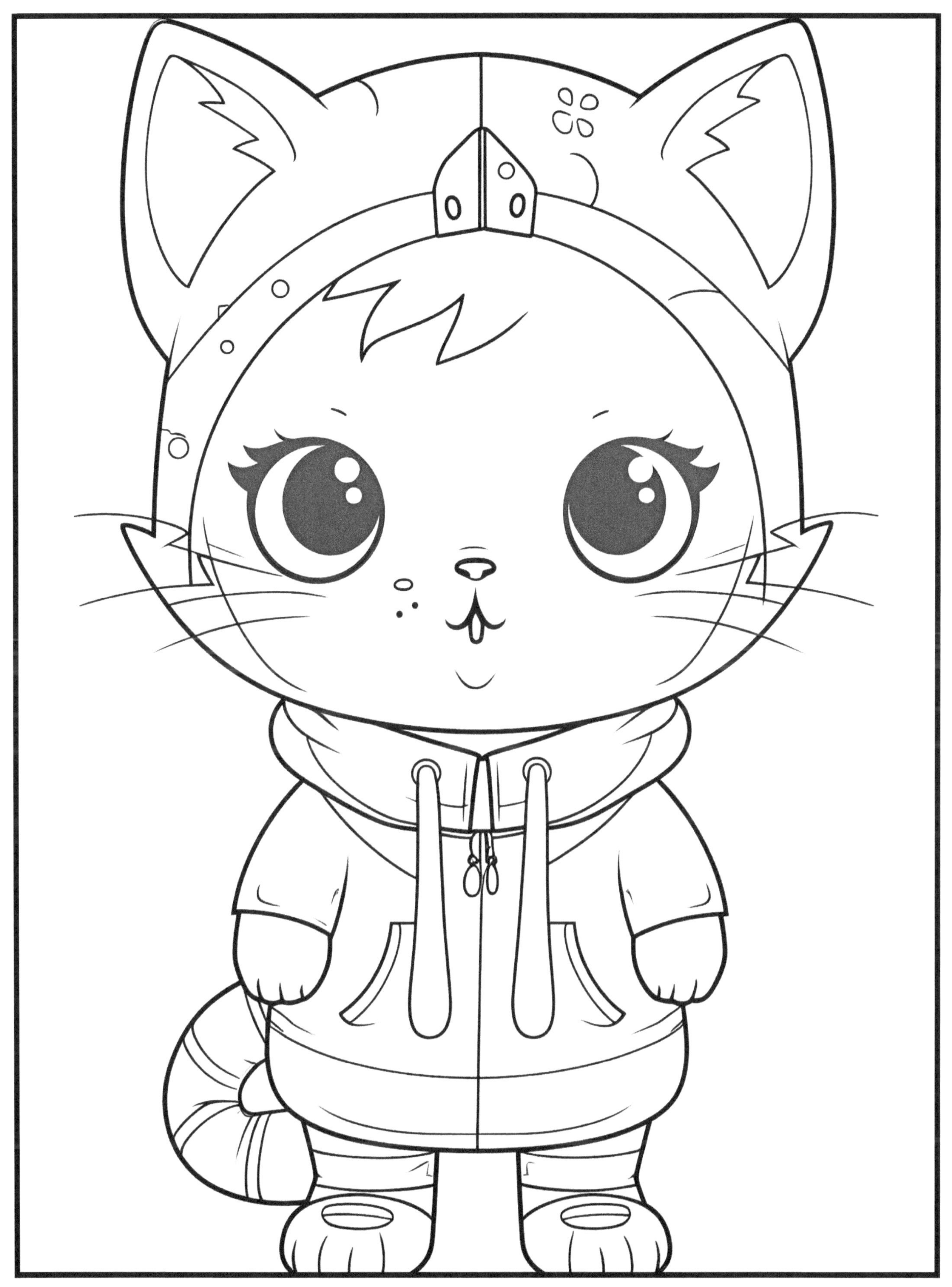

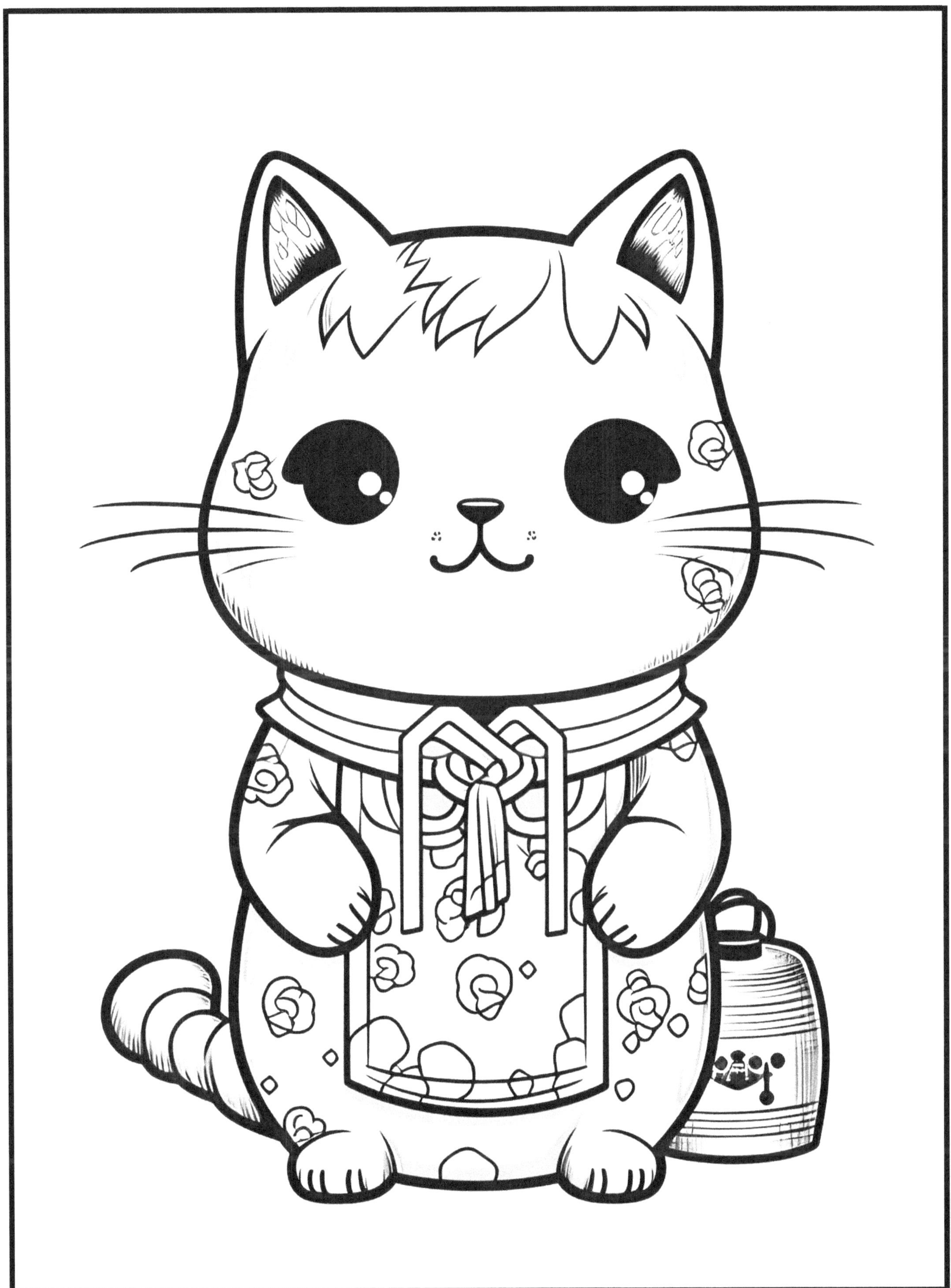

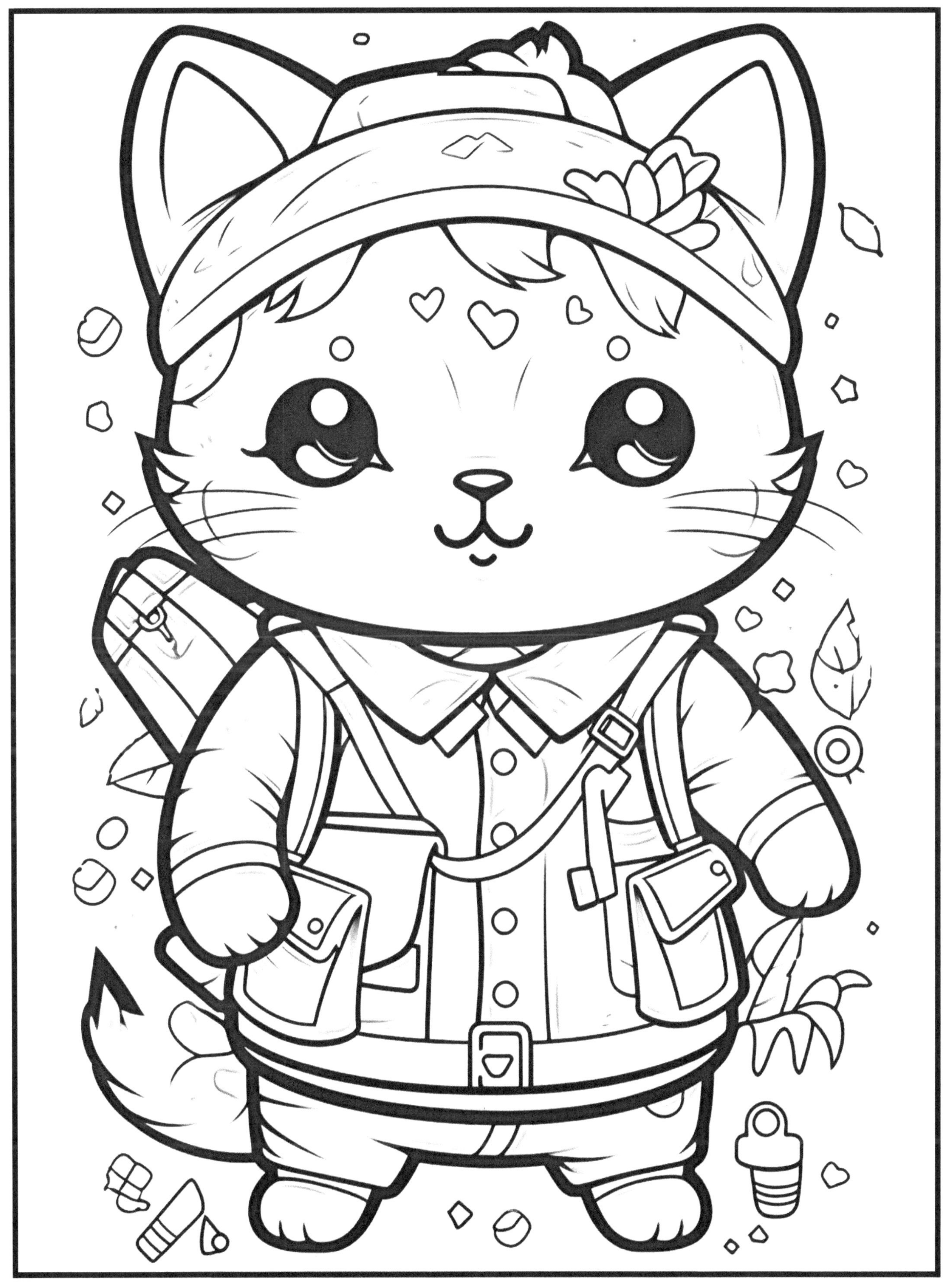

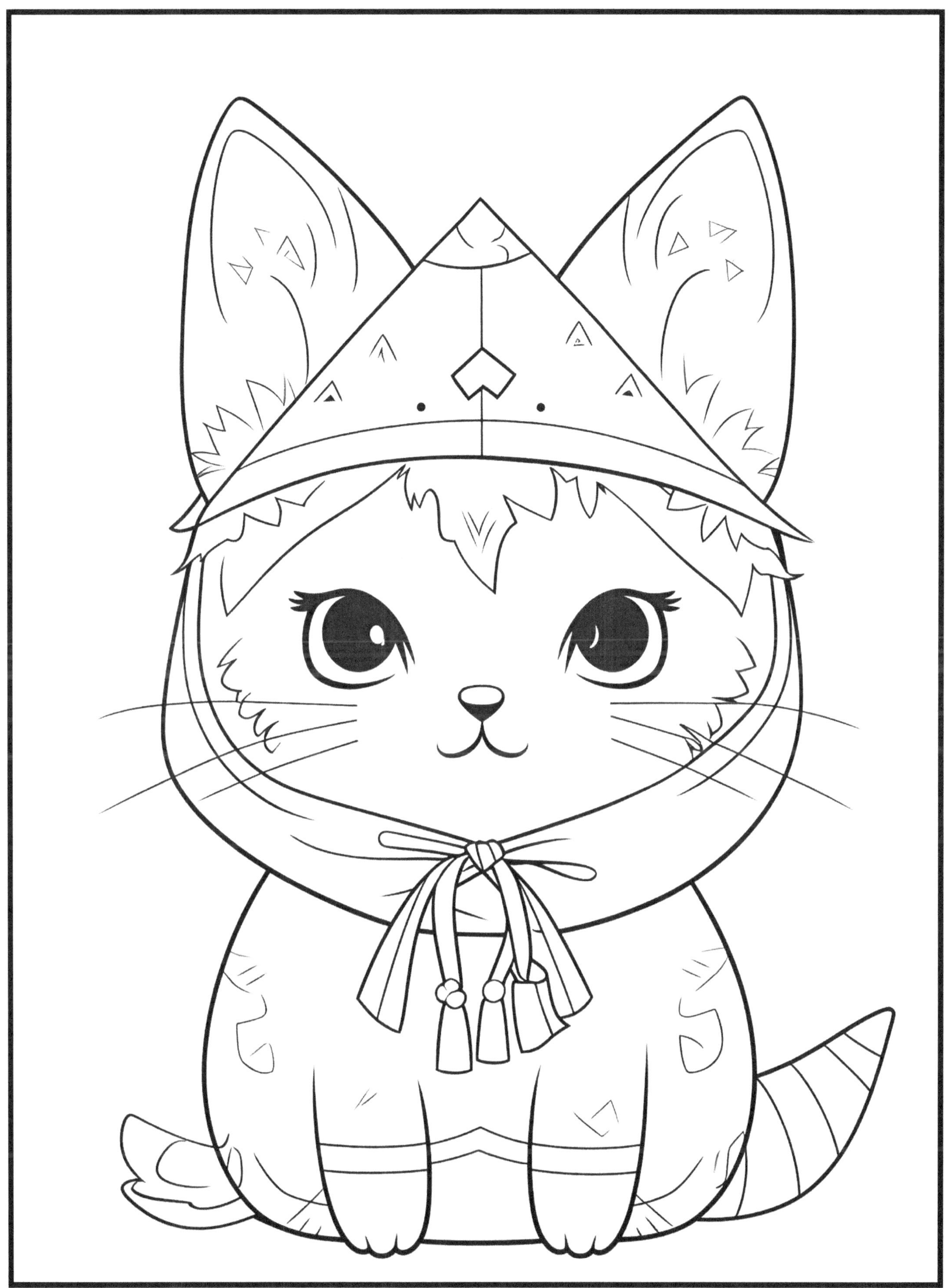

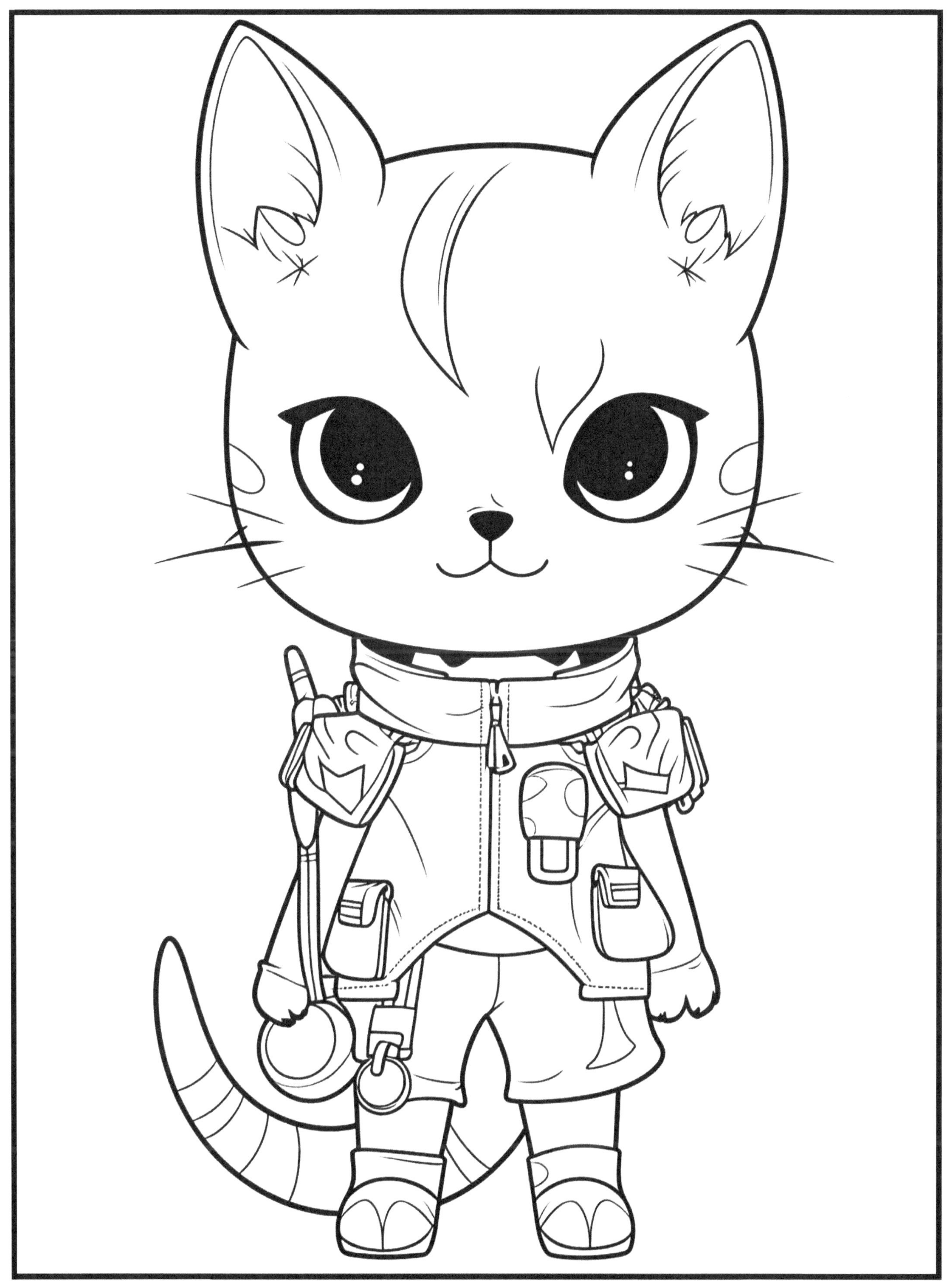

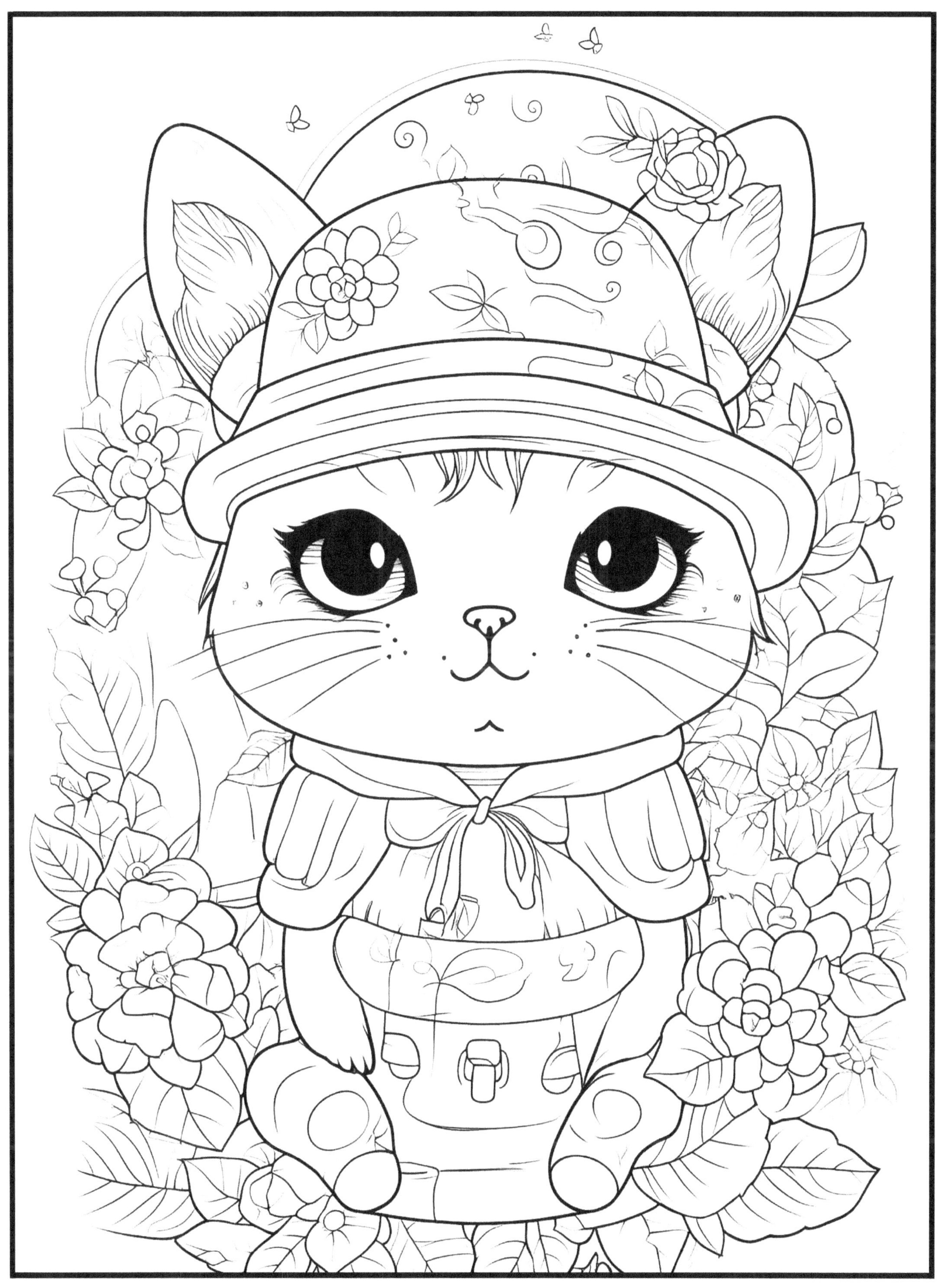

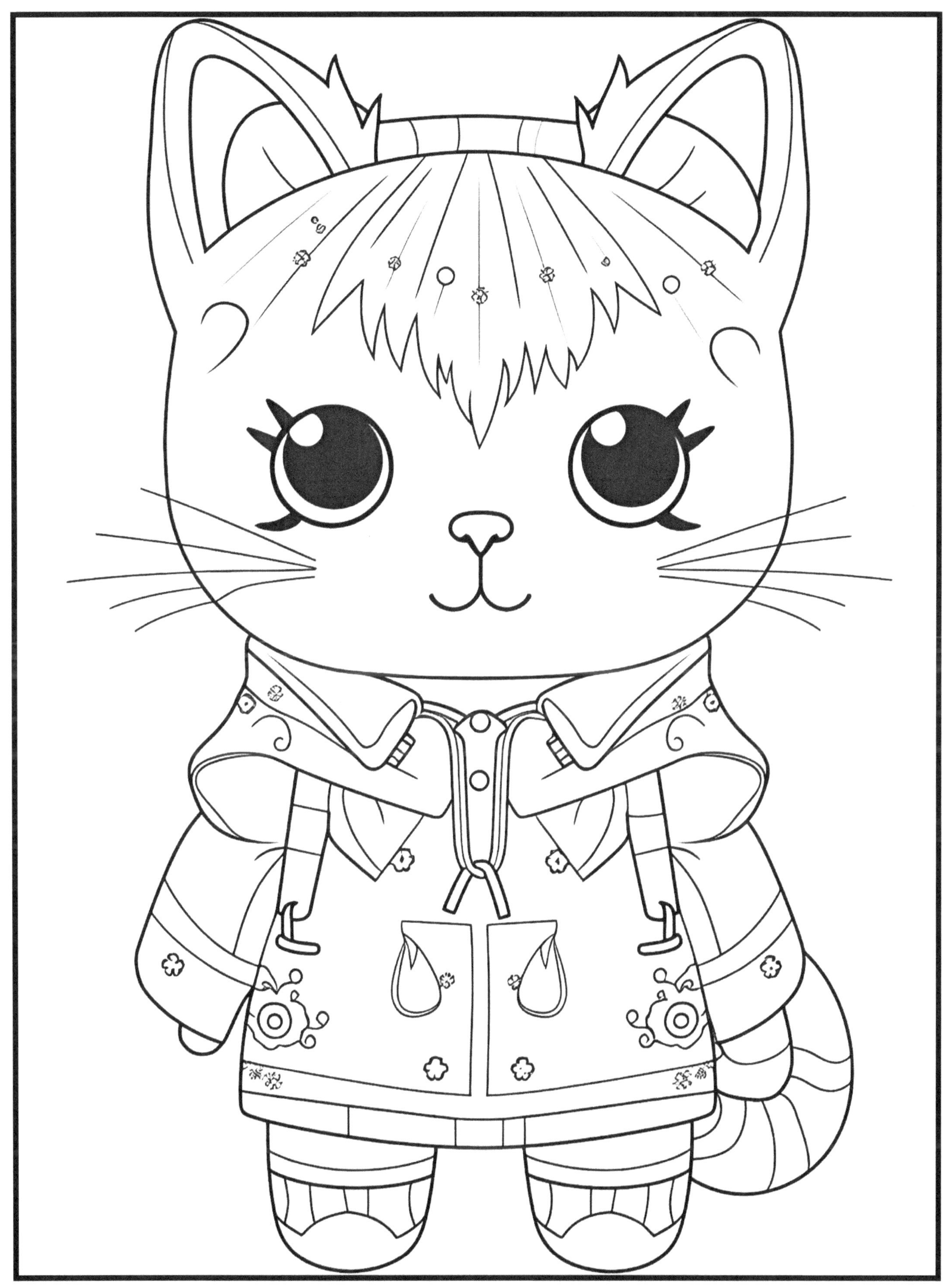

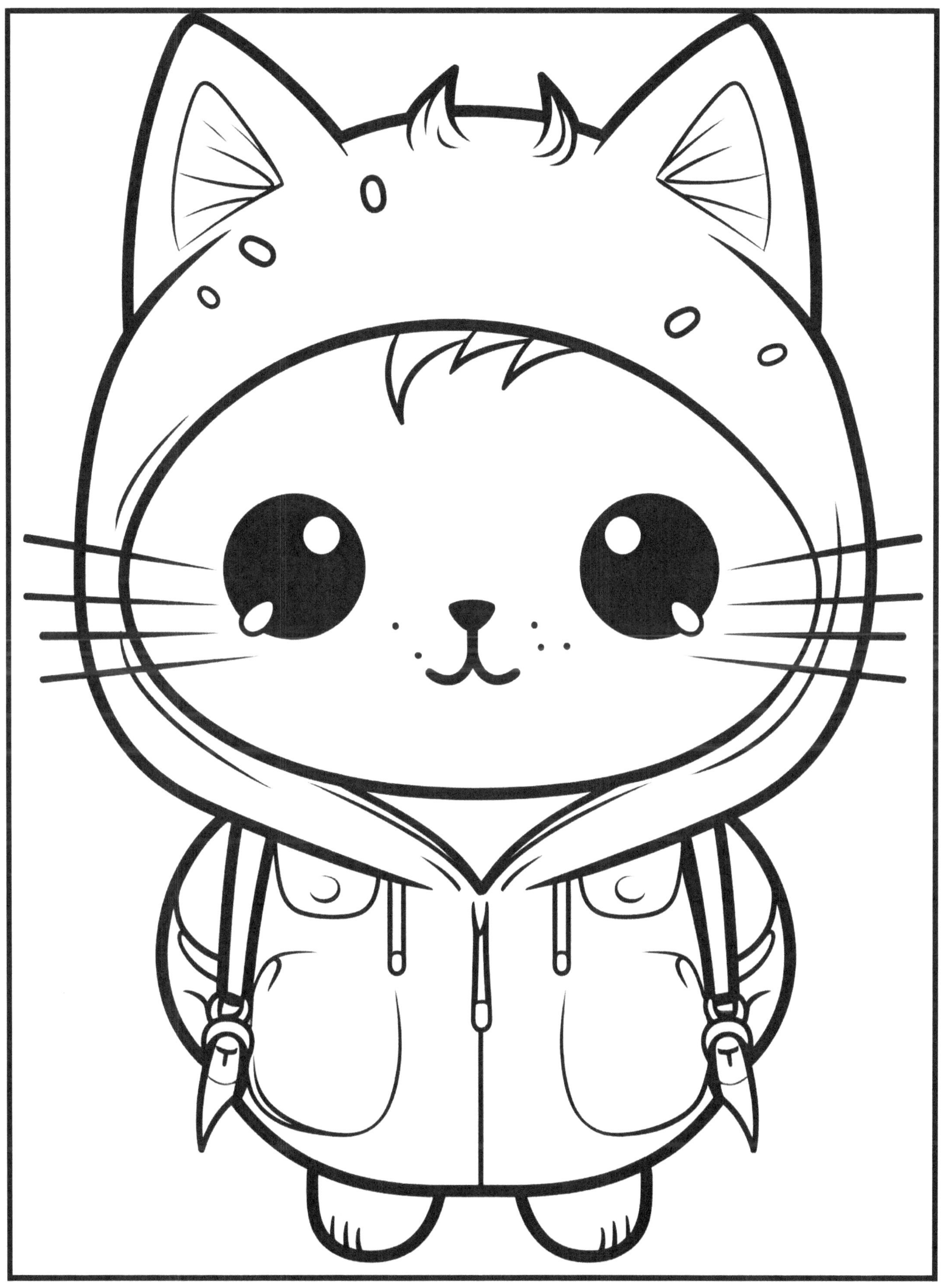

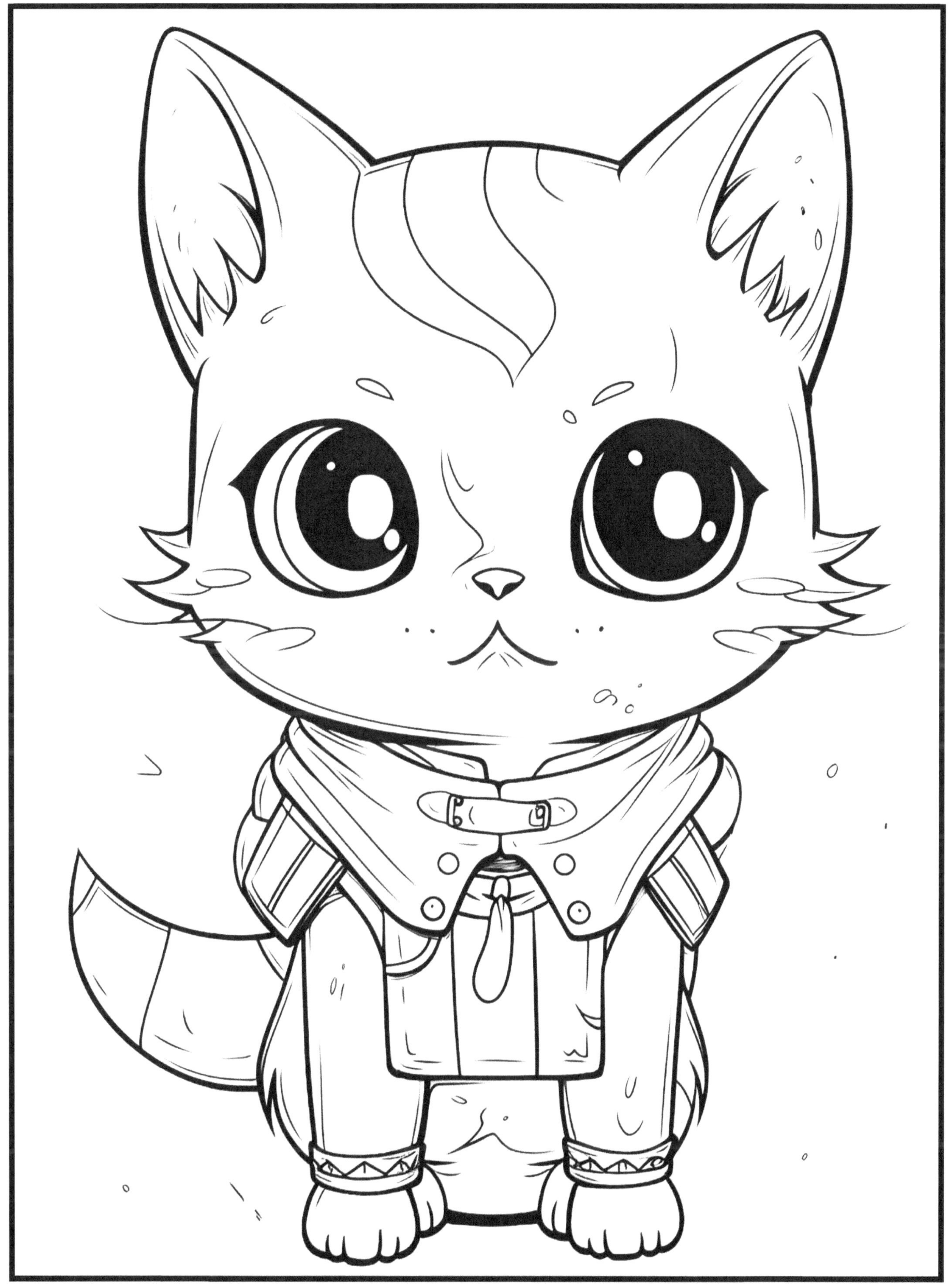

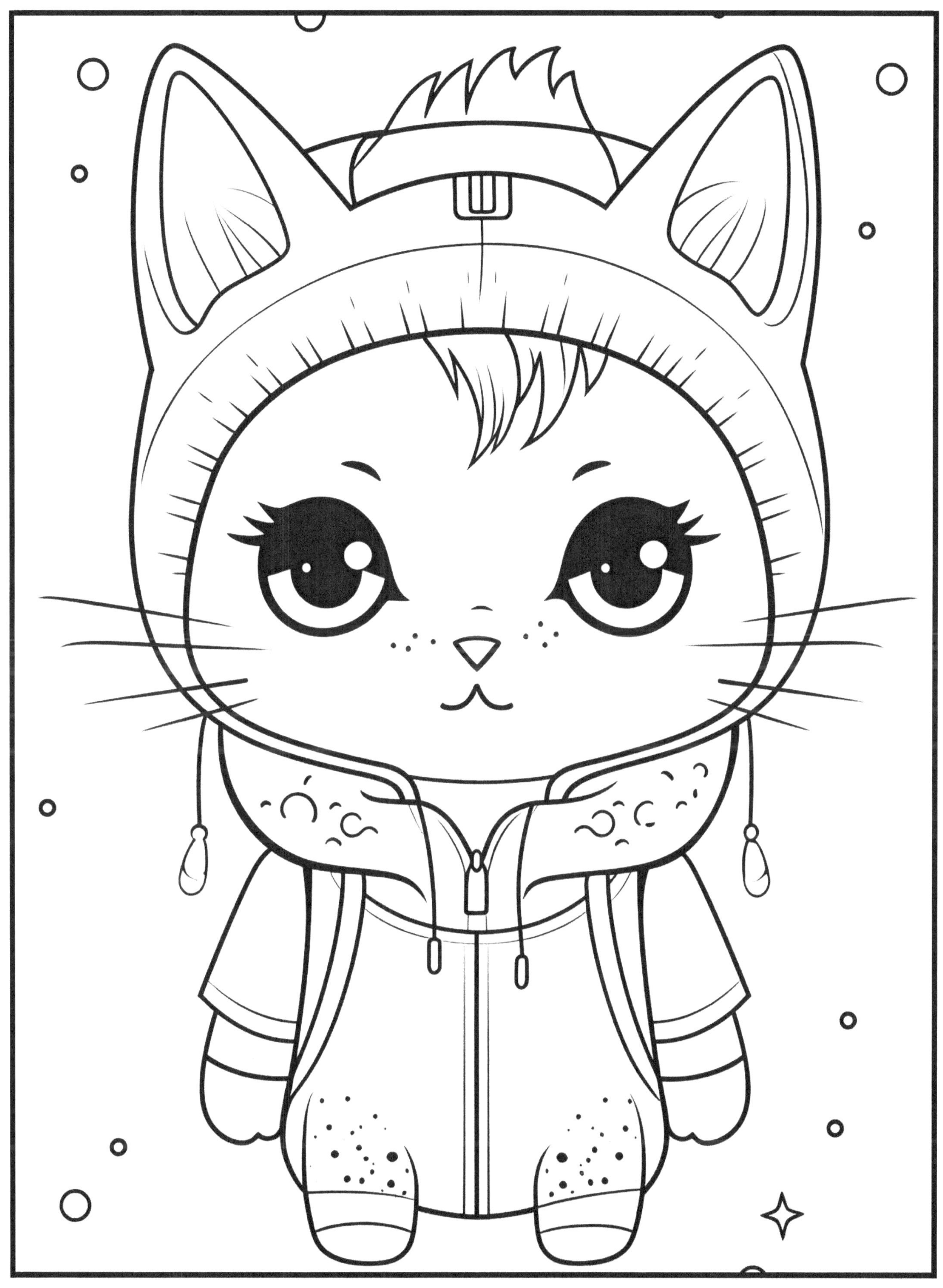

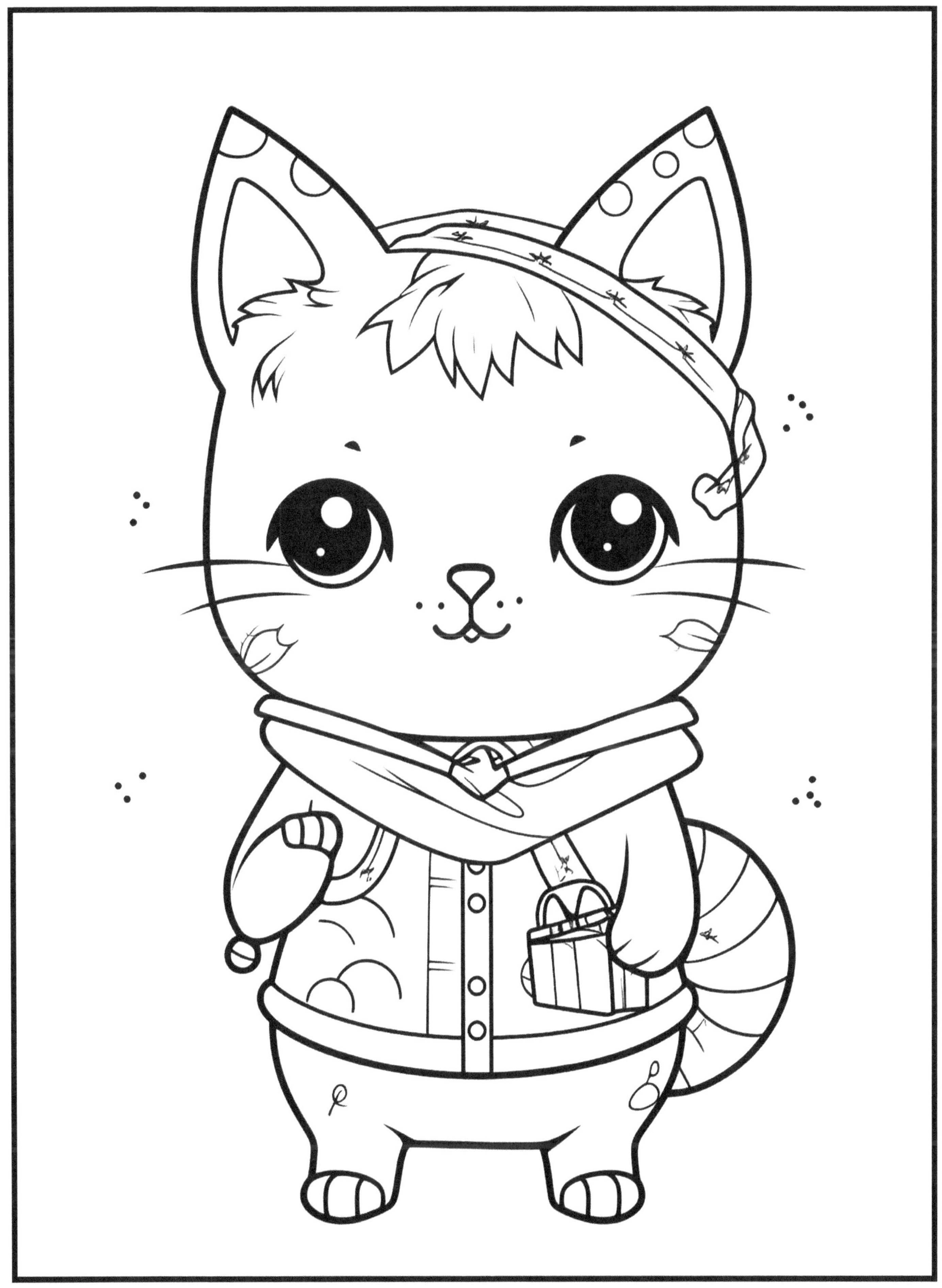

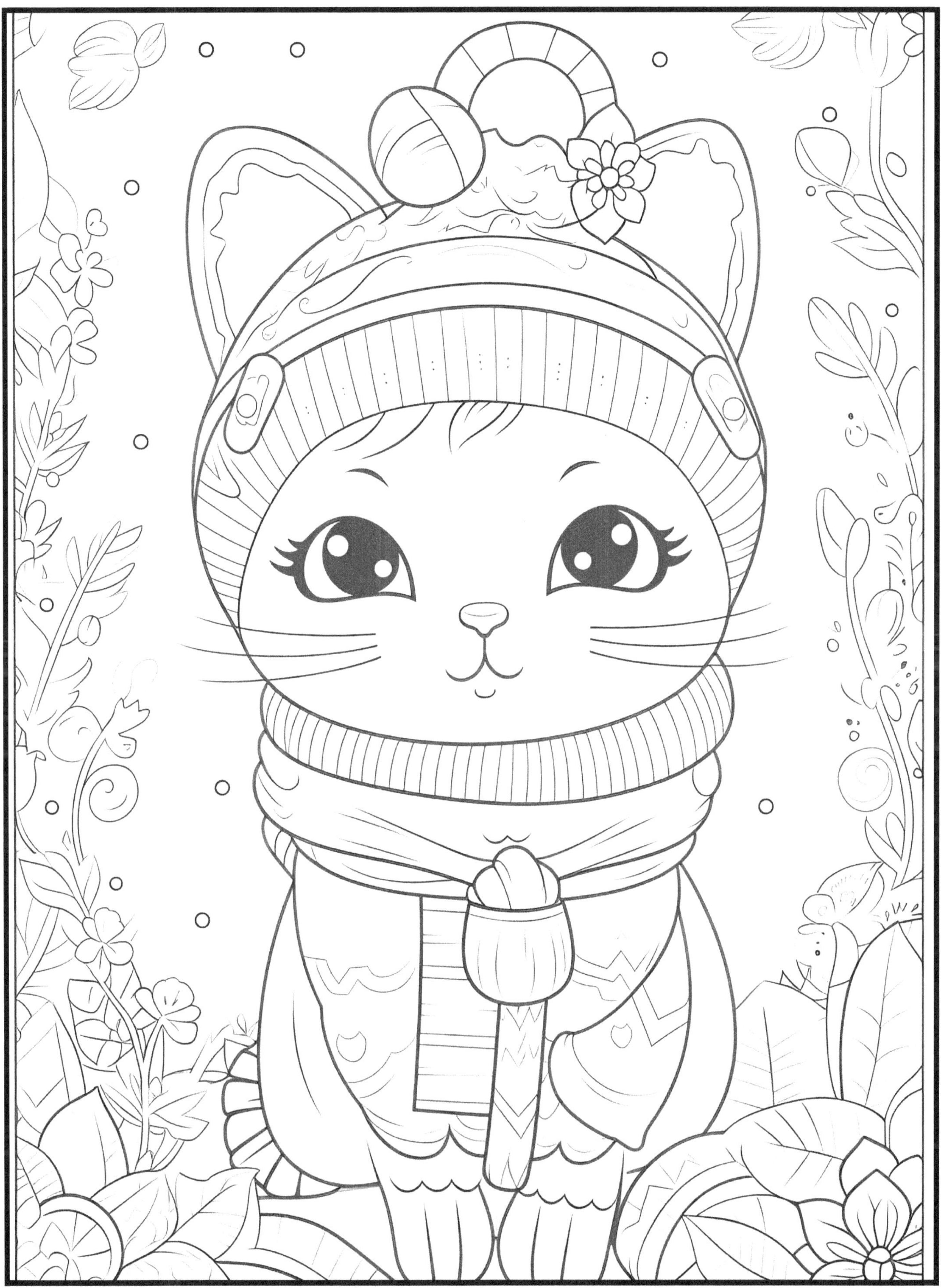

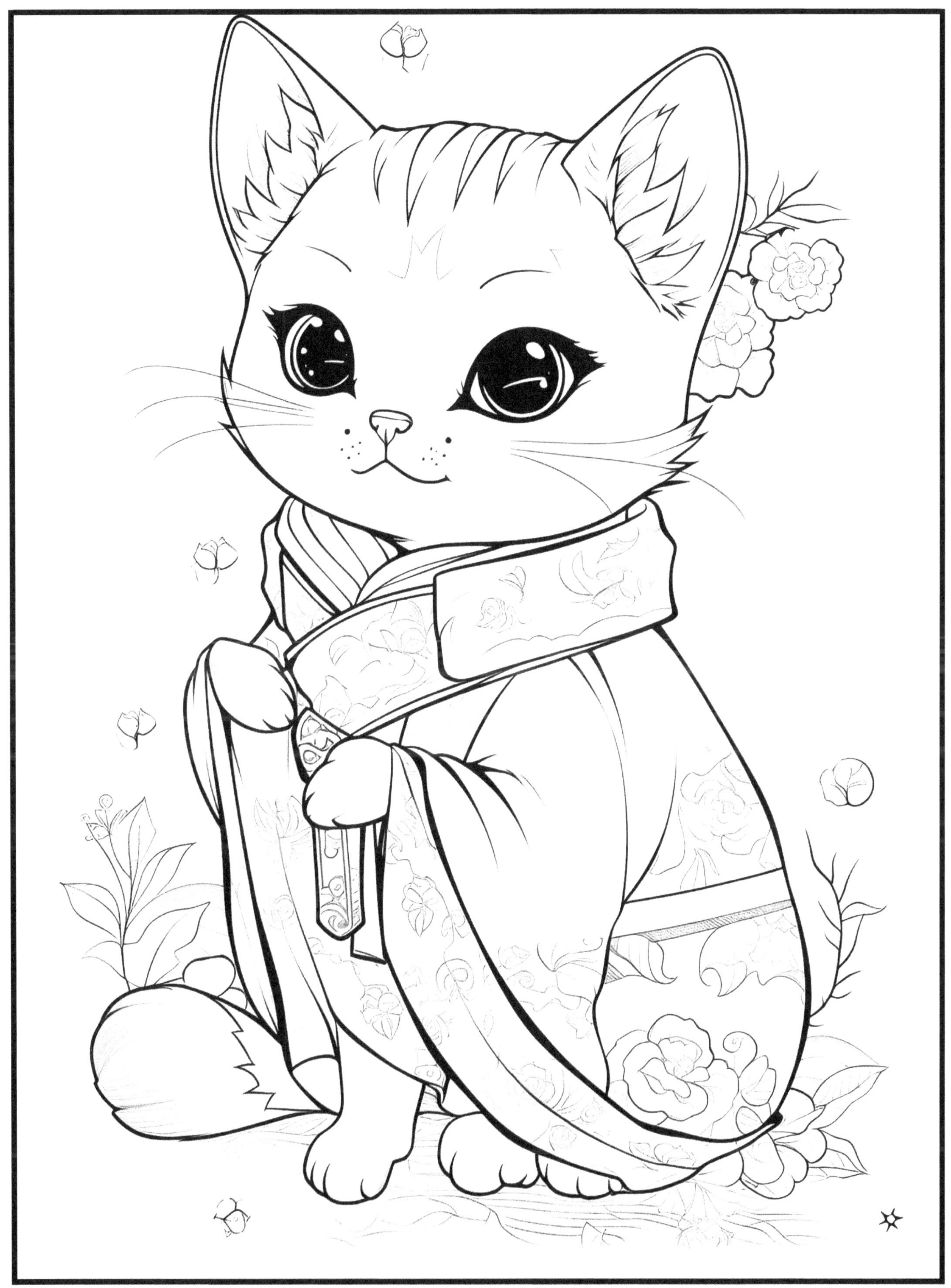

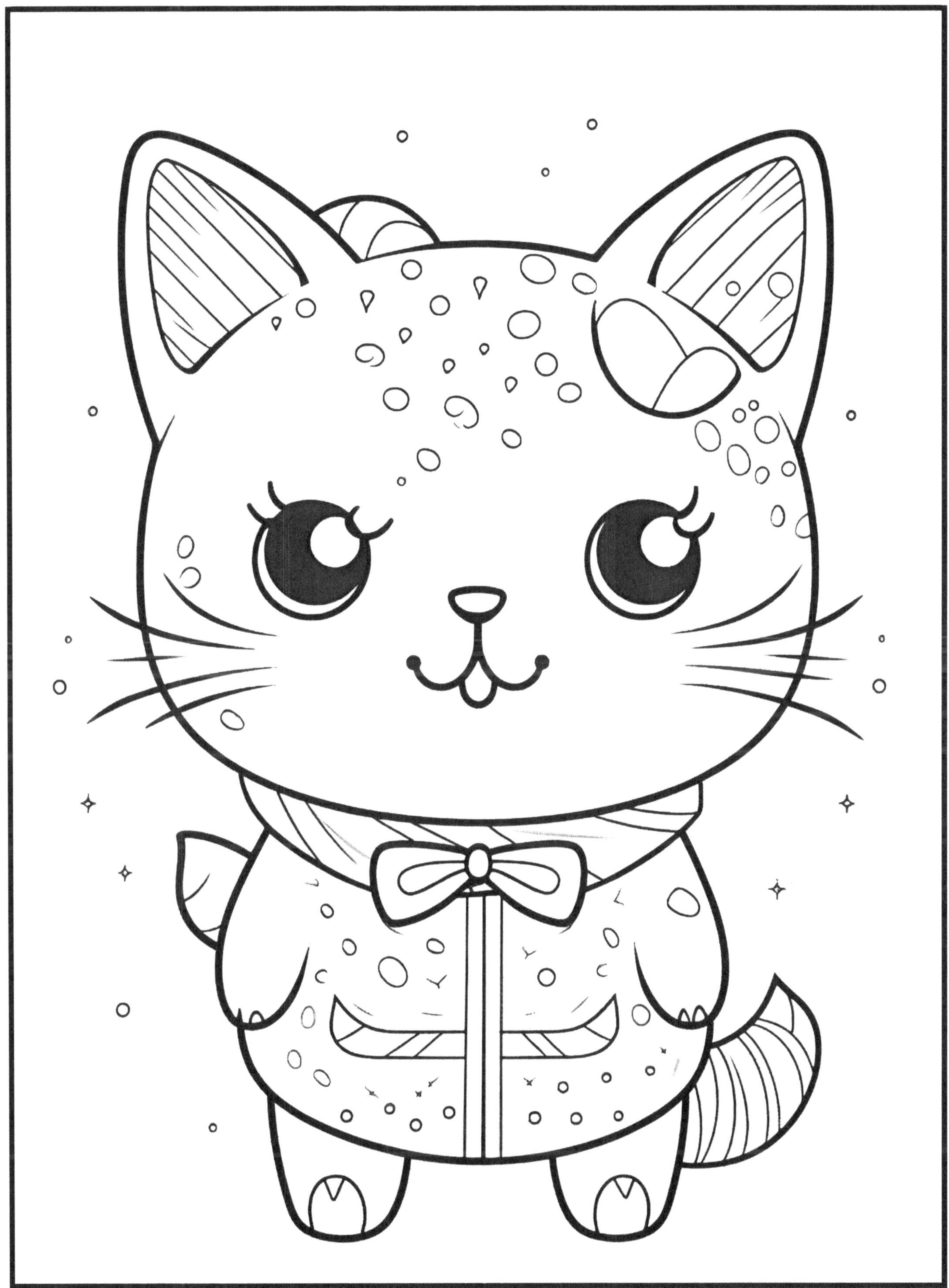

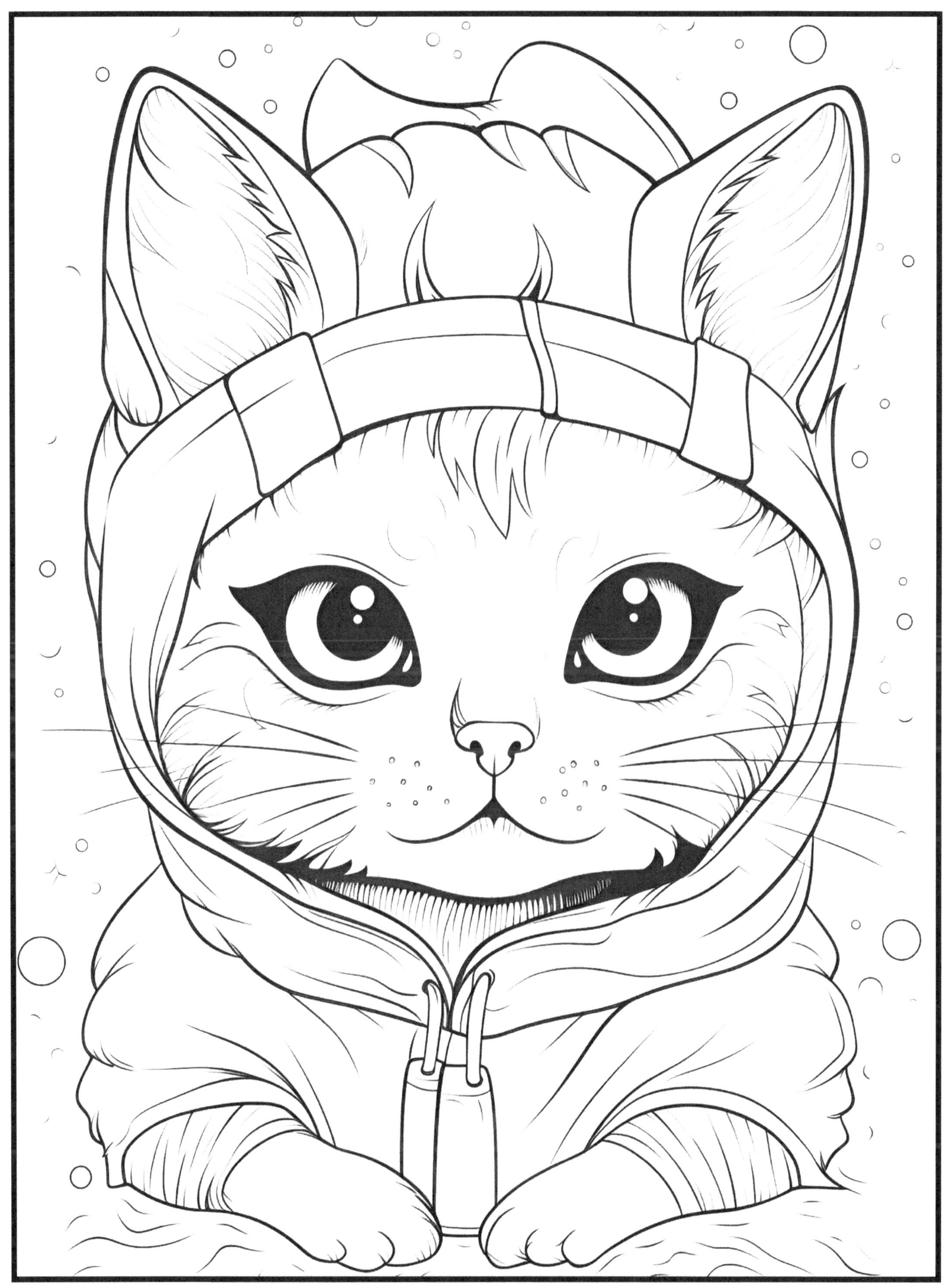

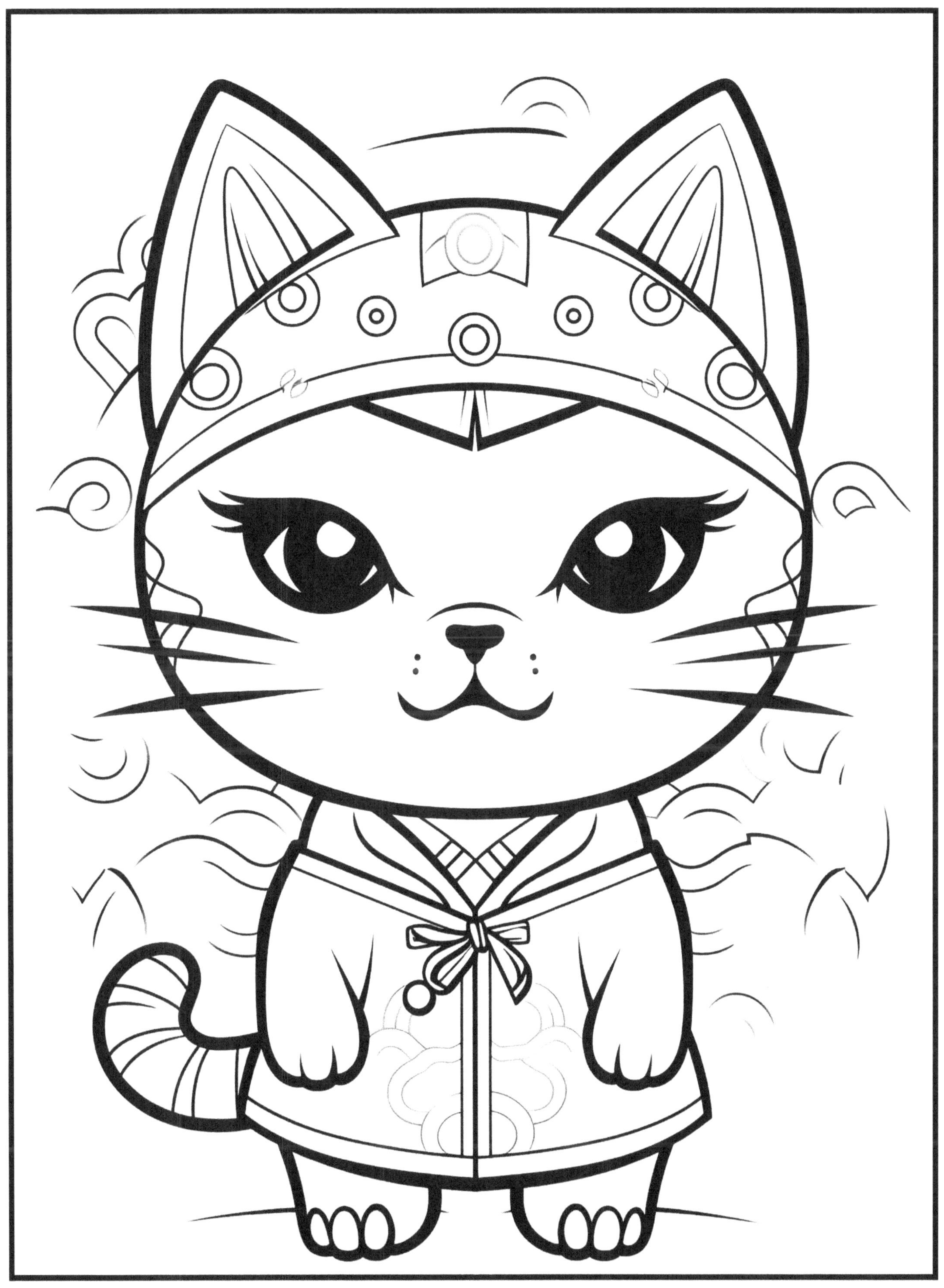

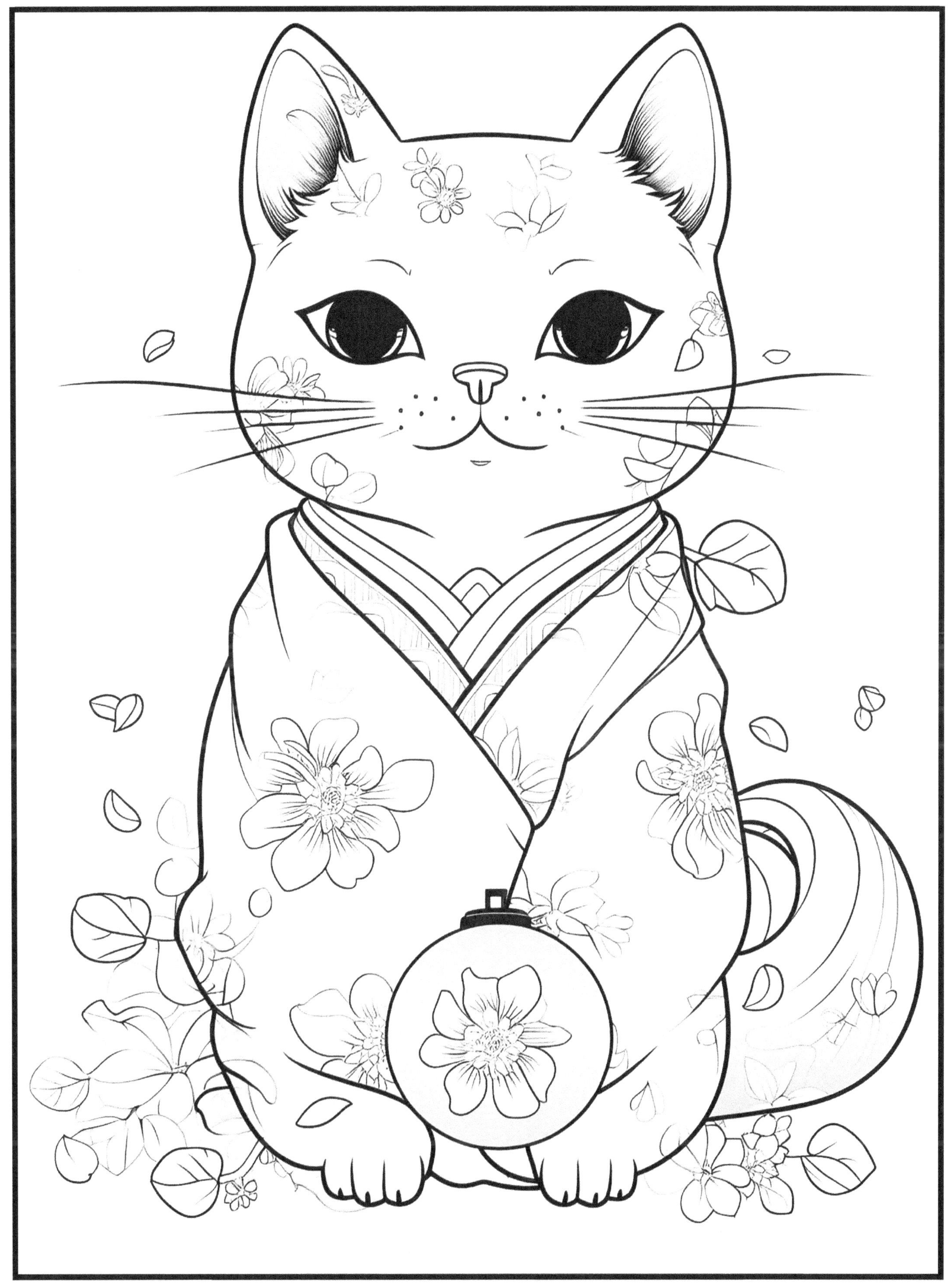

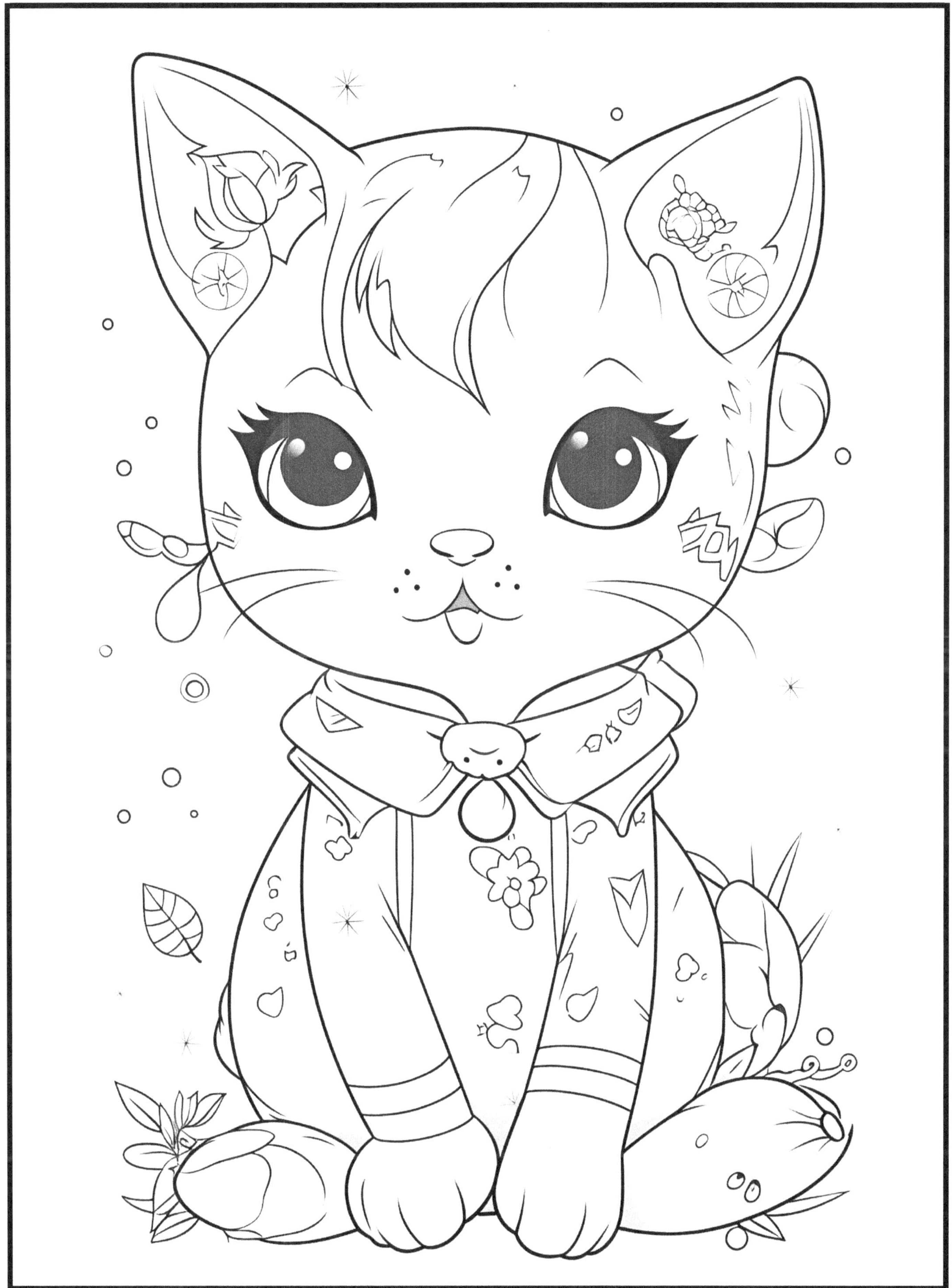

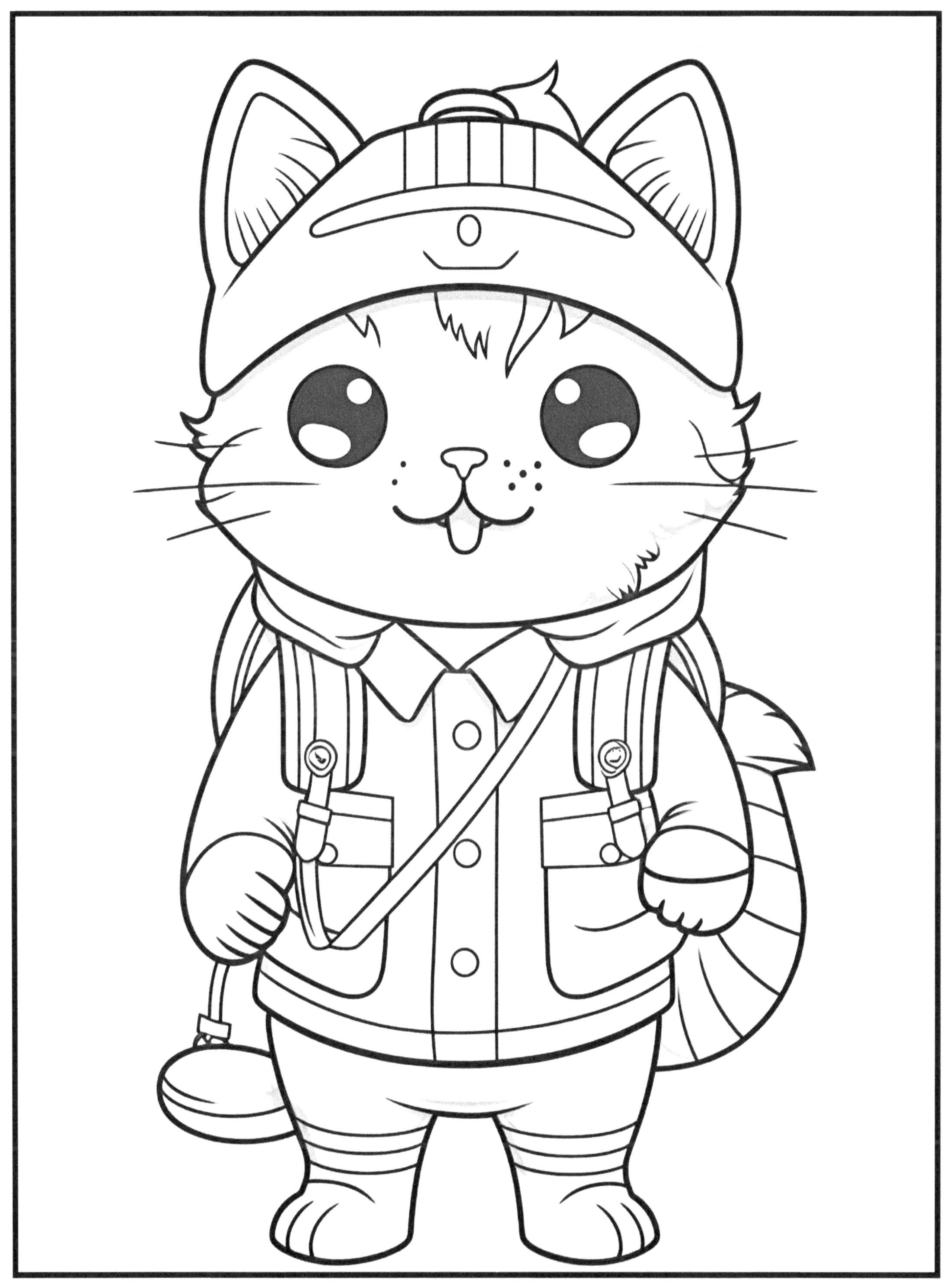

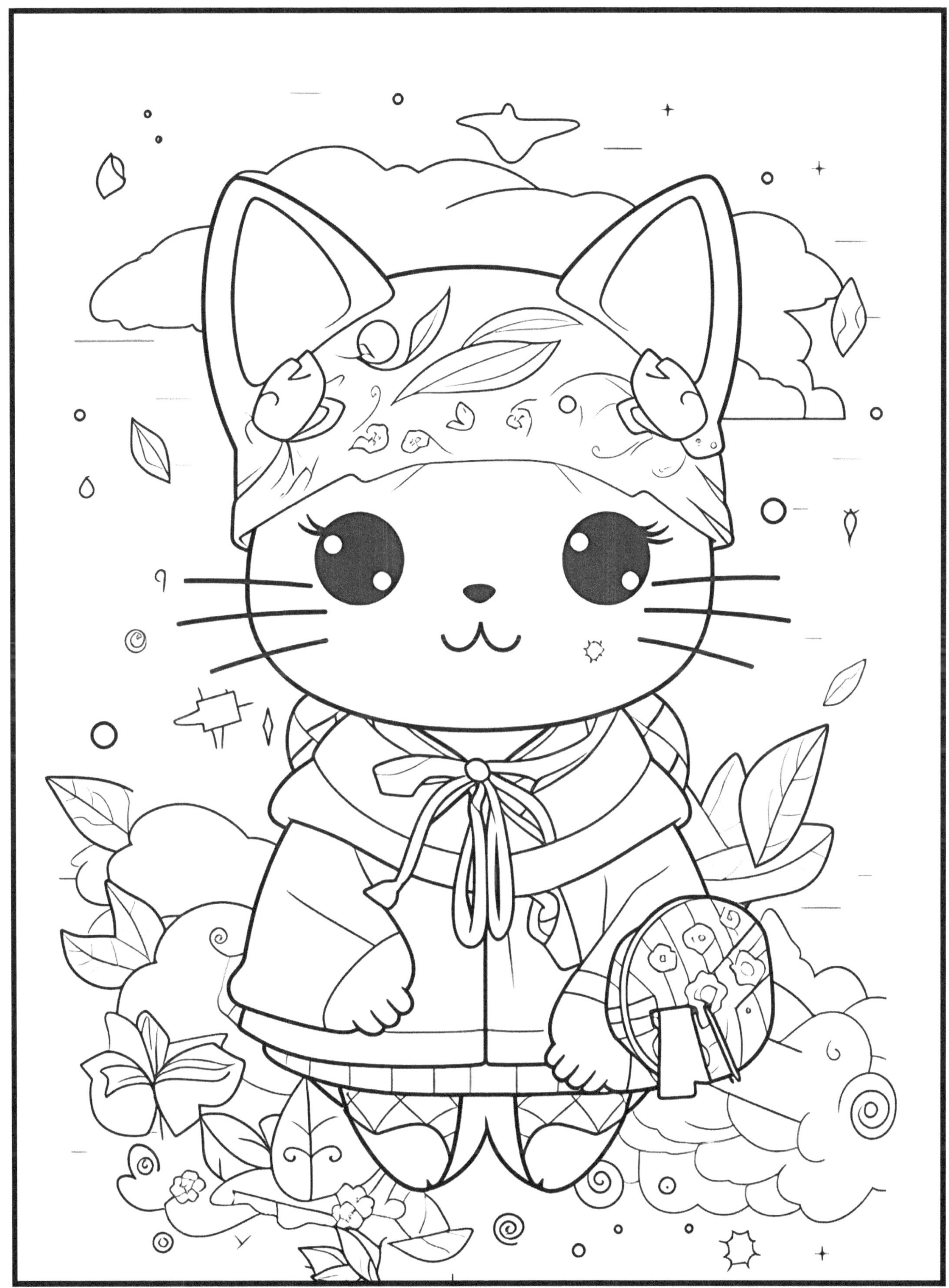

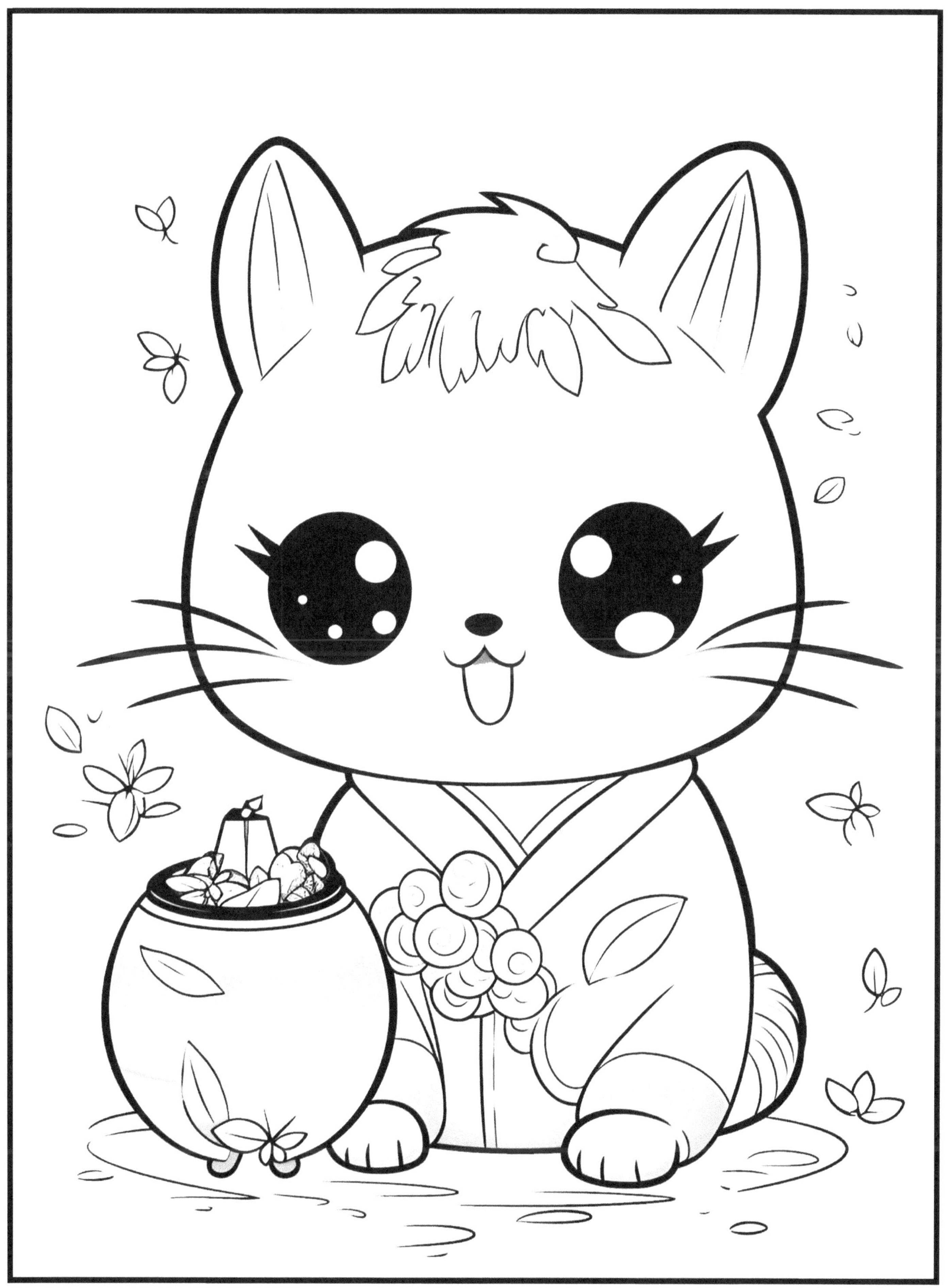

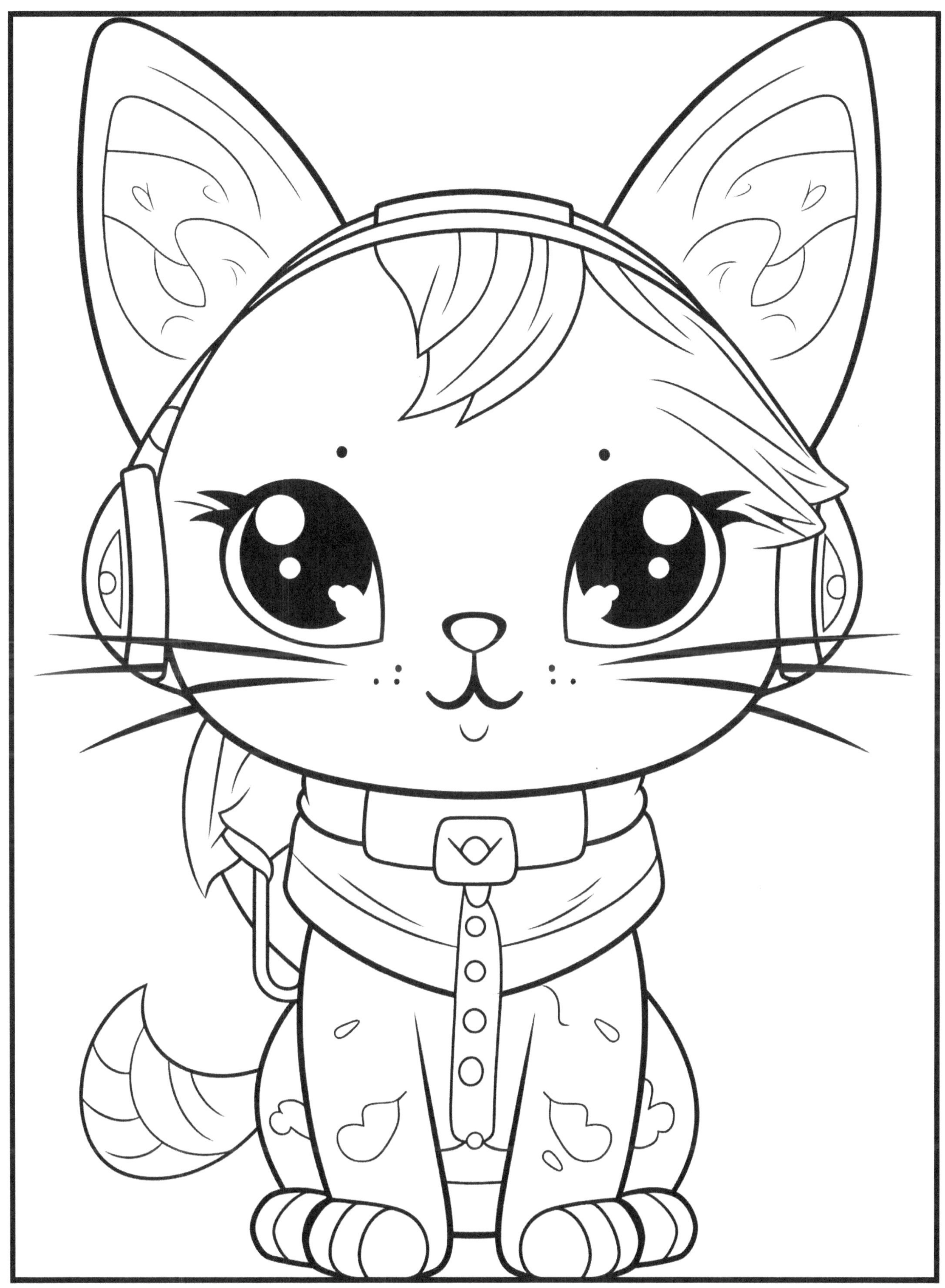

Love this Coloring book?
Want to show off your masterpiece?
Do you want your art displayed on our website?

1. Take a picture of a finished coloring page
2. Scan the QR Code to go to our website
3. Upload the photo of your finished coloring page

OR
Use #happytimesbooks or mention us @happytimesbooks on Instragram to have it displayed on our front page

No registration required

If you are under 18 please get a parents permission

https://happytimesbooks.com/pages/customer-art

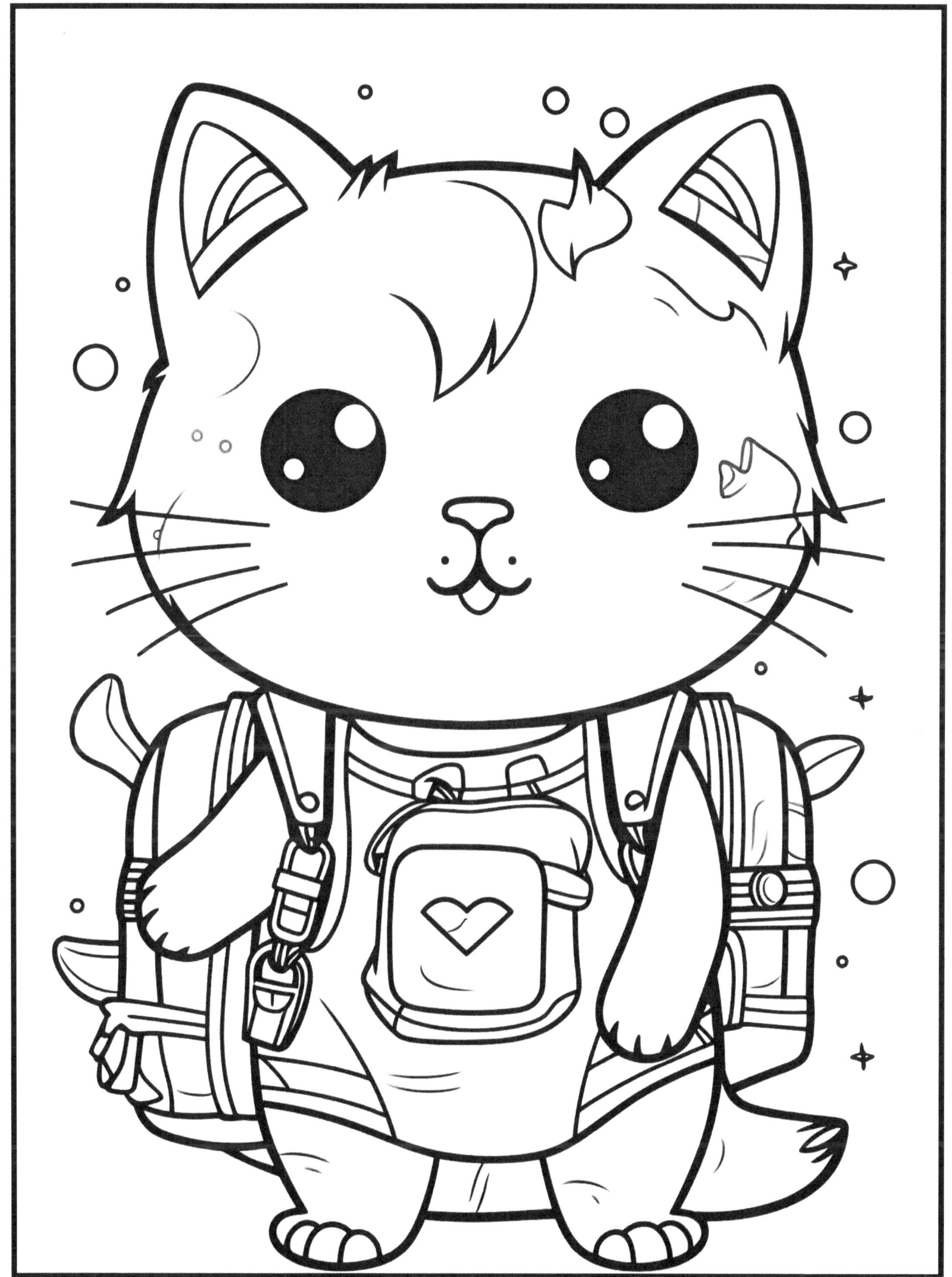

Love this Coloring book?
Want to show off your masterpiece?
Do you want your art displayed on our website?

1.   Take a picture of a finished coloring page
2.   Scan the QR Code to go to our website
3. Upload the photo of your finished coloring page

OR

Use #happytimesbooks or mention us @happytimesbooks on Instragram to have it displayed on our front page

No registration required

If you are under 18 please get a parents permission

https://happytimesbooks.com/pages/customer-art

Let's start on a numbers journey!

TEACHTIME's Early Math Workbook introduces your child to numeracy. By the end of the book they will know their numbers and be confidently adding and subtracting!

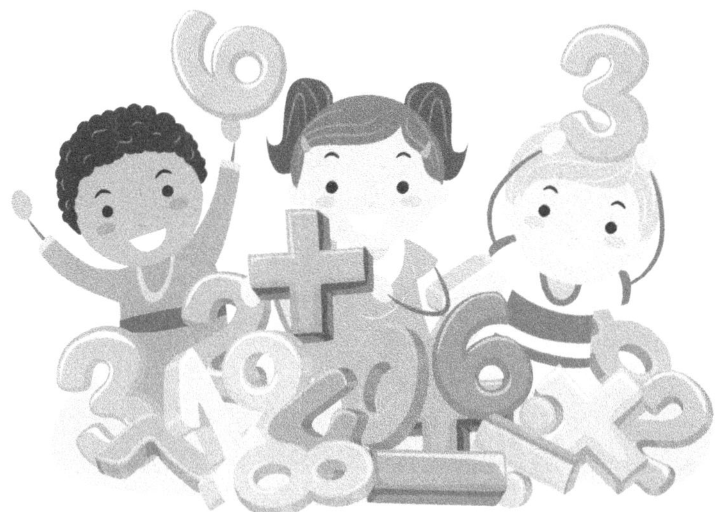

<u>What's inside this workbook?</u>

INTRODUCTION TO NUMBERS
First we learn each of the numbers from 1 to 20, We practice writing them out until they become second nature.

LET'S LEARN ADDITION
An introduction to the subject of addition. The simple visual learning method helps to teach the concept effectively.

ADDITION IN ACTION
Here we tackle a range of questions to test knowledge and build ability. We start off easy and progress to harder problems.

LET'S LEARN SUBTRACTION
The child is introduced to subtraction. The simple visual method helps to teach the concept effectively.

SUBTRACTION IN ACTION
We solve a number of questions to test knowledge and build skill. We begin easy and progres to harder problems.

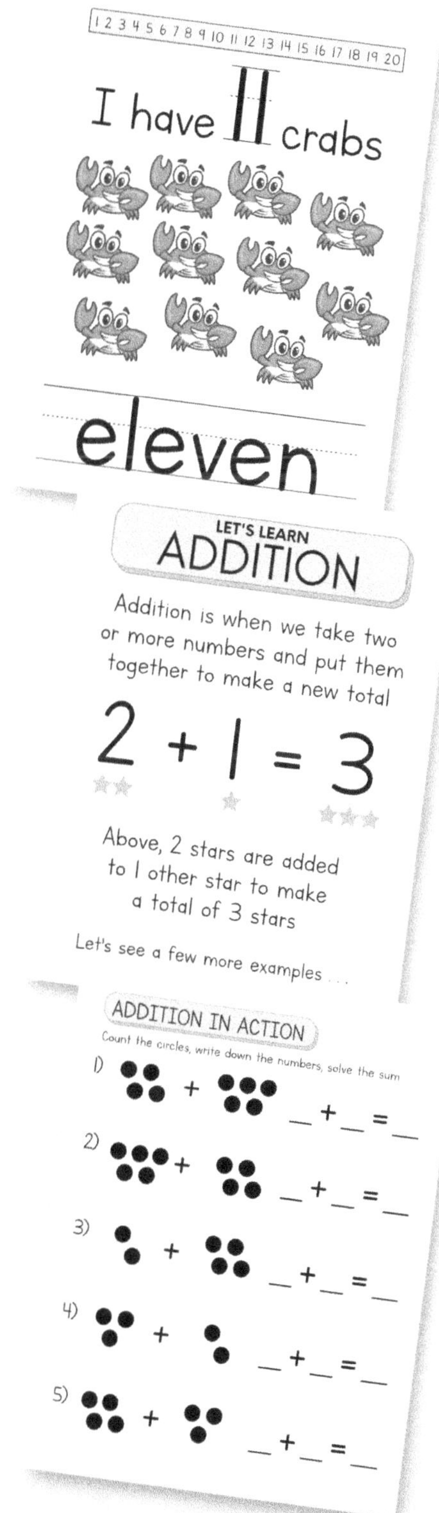

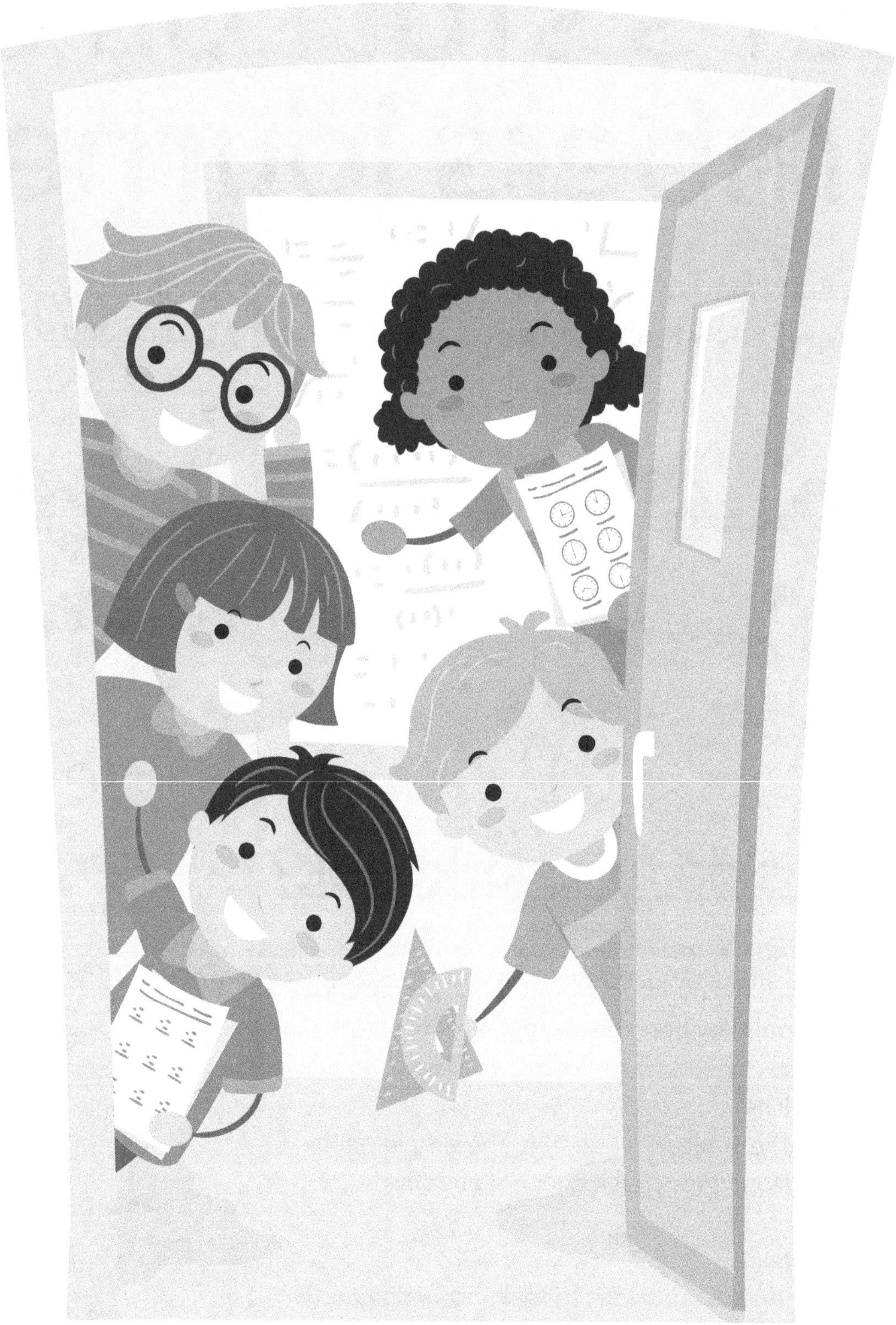

Note to parents: This workbook is designed so the child can work alone. An answers page has not been provided to avoid the child simply look up solutions. So we kindly ask parents to mark the work and give feedback.

We would be very grateful if you could leave a review of this book on Amazon